CONNECTING WHOLE-SCHOOL LITERACY

CONNECTING WHOLE-SCHOOL LITERACY

Building Capacity from Leadership to Classroom Practice

HAYLEY HARRISON

Published in 2025 by Amba Press, Melbourne, Australia
www.ambapress.com.au

© Hayley Harrison 2025

All rights reserved. No part of this book may be reproduced or transmitted in any form or by any means, electronic or mechanical, including photocopying, recording or by any information storage and retrieval system, without prior permission in writing from the publisher.

Cover design: Tess McCabe
Internal design: Amba Press
Editor: Rica Dearman

ISBN: 9781923403208 (pbk)
ISBN: 9781923403215 (ebk)

A catalogue record for this book is available from the National Library of Australia.

Dedication

To every teacher who has felt overwhelmed with the demands of literacy and the struggles students face in their classes.

To Trev, for giving just the right amount of support and space to allow such creations to occur.

Contents

Acknowledgements		1
About the author		3
Introduction		5
Chapter 1	Why every teacher is a literacy teacher	13
Chapter 2	Connecting vocabulary	37
Chapter 3	Connecting reading	73
Chapter 4	Connecting writing	107
Chapter 5	Leading whole-school literacy	143
Conclusion		183
References		187
List of figures and tables		191
Appendices		195
Index		197

Acknowledgements

This book might not have eventuated if it wasn't for Selena Prior, who had a vision for a reference book she could give to her undergraduate students to take with them to placement. She saw what I had achieved with *Connecting Literacy* and approached me to create 'the teacher version' that could bring everything together and provide clarification and strategies to action literacy learning and support within any classroom.

But it was Alicia Cohen at Amba Press who responded to my proposal, not only with enthusiasm and unwavering commitment, but with wisdom, guidance and a steadfast confidence that has been invaluable in my writing journey.

I must acknowledge all the teachers, leaders and schools I have worked with over the past 20 years, who have not only shaped me into the teacher I am today, but who have also trusted me enough to be honest and vulnerable in the questions they have asked and the concerns they've shared with me. I have written this text specifically for you: the teachers who so desperately want to help their students but struggle to reconcile their content understanding with the literacy demands they place upon their classes. This is for the teachers who simply don't have time to trawl through research or attend professional development that might fill gaps uncovered from teacher training. This is for the teachers who are forced to attend one of my literacy workshops and come up to me afterwards, admitting: "I thought that was going to be another total waste of time, but now I'm wondering if you have anything I can refer back to as I try some of these things out." And this is for all the Literacy, Curriculum and Faculty Leaders who are working tirelessly to make genuine and lasting change across their school, but don't quite know where to start, how to build upon what they have begun, or how to bring all the pieces they've considered together.

More personally, I would like to thank Paul Carter, Elizabeth Harrison, Amy Hempel and Selena Prior, who so willingly agreed to read and engage in the initial drafts of the manuscript, and who were all critical in the success and clarity of the final product.

Finally, I must thank my husband, Trevor, and my boys, who not only have accepted my moments of hyper-focused writing, but have also supported my decision to take on significant projects, such as this, alongside the plethora of chaos and activities that richly fill our lives.

About the author

Hayley Harrison is a teacher, consultant, tutor, cycle instructor, wife and mum (not necessarily in that priority order). She is the founder of *Connect Literacy*, a consulting organisation specialising in literacy, curriculum development and mentoring school leaders. Hayley has spent her career teaching in secondary classrooms and working alongside English faculties, classroom teachers and educational leaders across Australia to understand the literacy demands of their subject and the ways they can explicitly teach, support, consolidate, transfer and extend student literacy skills and build confidence in the context of their school.

In 2023, her first passion project, *Connecting Literacy*, was published through Matilda Education. This sequenced collection of student folios and teacher reference guides elevates the traditional English skills book into a text that prioritises the transference of literacy knowledge into numerous text forms and purposes, while supporting teachers through the research of how to teach literacy concepts in explicit, embedded and authentic ways.

Hayley has also authored both the *VCE English and EAL Units 3 + 4* and *VCE English and EAL Units 1 + 2* textbooks through Matilda Education and continues to run student writing and exam workshops across Victoria.

Her next adventure, between her continued work with schools and facilitating staff workshops, is to bring to life her vision of a text she always wanted to exist when she started teaching English. Tentatively titled *The English Teacher's Guide to Understanding and Teaching Grammar*, she can't wait to continue the journey of turning her passion and experience into words on the page that hopefully go towards making teachers' lives that tiny bit easier *and* effective.

Introduction

My husband regularly looks at me and shakes his head, saying, "I've never known anyone who loves their job as much as you." Yet, I've had the privilege of working with innumerable teachers over the past 20 years who are so passionate about what they do each day that I never feel alone in my passion for everything there is to learn about teaching literacy.

But just because you love something, doesn't make it easy.

Working with teenagers has never been a walk in the park, and with an increasingly fast-paced world – full of distractions, temptations, injustices and changing expectations – it's little wonder teachers are feeling overwhelmed, disenchanted and deeply concerned for the future.

I'm not saying that reading this book will fix all that. But I do genuinely believe that #literacysaveslives and #literacymatters, and when we gift students with the ability to read deeply, purposefully and meaningfully, and with the ability to write accurately, articulately and confidently, then we are able to set future generations up with some of the most essential tools they will need to navigate successfully through life.

Unfortunately, many literacy resources are designed for the primary years of education. And this makes sense. If we can teach literacy properly from the beginning, we have a much greater capacity to extend student thinking and skills in more critical and sophisticated ways once they enter high school. In this idyllic world, every student would come into Year 7 having the ability to read and comprehend grade-level texts, and articulate their understanding with grade-level vocabulary that uses accurate and increasingly sophisticated spelling, grammar and punctuation – expressed through legible handwriting, no less!

But this is, too often, not a reality. Most high school classrooms can expect up to eight years of difference in skills and knowledge between their weakest and strongest students, and many schools are finding an increasing number of their Year 7 cohort arriving with Year 5 (or below!) literacy skills. The genuine need to 'fill' student literacy gaps has somehow become a priority in an already insanely overcrowded curriculum.

Yet, secondary teachers are (often) not educated in **foundational literacy skills*** or ways to support students working with primary school level literacy. Where are teachers supposed to find the time to go back and teach spelling concepts or handwriting, or the fact that a sentence is supposed to start with a capital letter? And whose responsibility is this? Secondary teachers are specialists in their subject area, but do they now need to be literacy specialists, too?

Add to this, literacy is complex.

We can talk about improving students' reading and writing, but there are so many skills required to read and write that it is not as simple as finding a program or strategy to 'fix' reading or writing. Rather, literacy support requires an *understanding* of potential issues, and the *strategies* to navigate these issues through scaffolding reading and writing demands purposefully.

Sure, this may sound plausible in theory, but when there are already so many competing priorities in any given school day, who possibly has the time and energy to process, experiment with and embed something as complex as literacy?

---

* **Foundational literacy skills:** the mechanics required to read and write.

I have worked in so many different school contexts; with so many different teachers from different faculties, with different experiences and confidence levels; with so many different students from every walk of life. I have seen what is possible. By synthesising my experience and understanding, I have attempted to bring a resource together that not only explains the impact literacy has across subject areas but explains some of the best strategies and activities I've seen work to support and extend any student a teacher might find in their class now and into the future.

How to make the most of this resource

For the classroom teacher

I've tried to balance the text, so you can build from the facts (the research and understanding we have around teaching and supporting literacy for adolescents) into the practical applications of this research and understanding in the classroom.

Chapter 1 sets up the rationale and importance of literacy for every teacher. This chapter explores the complexity of literacy alongside the necessity for every teacher to understand the literacy demands of their subject. I acknowledge oral literacy in this initial chapter and provide some classroom strategies to promote effective speaking and listening skills. Ultimately, the chapter lays the foundation for what you need to do with the information moving forward.

Chapters 2, 3 and 4 work through a similar structure of establishing the theory around how people build their vocabulary, learn to read or learn to write, before considering the demands students face with new vocabulary, reading or writing tasks across any given day. Various classroom examples are provided alongside strategies and skills to consider for all subject areas. Each chapter concludes with five relevant activities, along with specific examples of what it might look like to engage with these skills in your classroom.

Throughout each chapter, the 'Questions to Connect' encourage you to stop and connect with the information that has been provided and consider its relevance and impact within the context of the subjects and cohorts you teach. The more you allow yourself to pause, reflect and engage with these questions, the better you will be able to process how to turn the words on the page into actions in your classroom.

Towards the end of each chapter, the 'Connect: from page to practice' activities present ways to action the information that has been presented throughout the chapter. Ideally, these actions would be undertaken in faculty teams or referenced with the time and space for collaborative discussion, resource building and curriculum planning. It is one thing to read and understand the text – but it doesn't fulfil its purpose if you don't then turn the information into actions that impact your teaching in positive ways.

The final page of every chapter is a visual summary of the key elements of the chapter. This can be downloaded and used as a poster or support resource to help you consolidate and visually remind you of the elements you've explored throughout.

For the leaders

While the first four chapters are written for any classroom teacher to engage with, the final chapter is written specifically for those of you who have literacy in your leadership portfolio. You may be the Literacy Leader, the Teaching and Learning Leader, the Principal/Director or any number of leadership roles that encompass the teaching and learning of literacy. Whether you are at the very beginning or in the thick of tackling the beast that is literacy development, I'm hoping Chapter 5 will help provide some clarity in ways to purposefully move forward and maximise the precious time and energy available to you.

Change in a school takes time, so it is important to prioritise setting everything up properly (even if that takes longer than you would like!), rather than rush into random professional development or changes to the curriculum if you don't know where you are going.

Chapter 5 will guide you through ways to:

- Audit your current situation
- Draft a Literacy Framework
- Establish priorities
- Backwards map these into a workable Action Plan.

It would be beneficial to then consider how you might embed the use of this text to support you (and your teachers) moving forward.

I've written the 'Questions to Connect' in such a way that you could present elements from the chapter in a staff workshop and then use the questions as reflective tasks and activities for your teams. Remember, you don't want to move too quickly and overwhelm or overload your teachers – one chapter's content might take any number of sessions to move through properly.

The 'Connect: from page to practice' activities are written in a way for faculty or subject teams to engage purposefully with the content of each chapter. As the leader, you might initially work with the Faculty Leaders to upskill them in the content and then allow them to lead their teams through the activities. Or you might begin by leading the explicit teaching of information with the whole staff and then ask Faculty Leaders to continue this work in their teams more specifically. There are also numerous downloadable resources in the appendices (page 195) for you to gift to and support your teachers with along the way.

In this way, I'm asking you to consider: the scope and sequencing of literacy knowledge; engagement with curriculum, potential resources and assessment; and the application of literacy teaching and learning into the classroom – just like we ask our teachers to engage with the teaching and learning of the skills and knowledge in their classes.

This book (and Chapter 5 in particular) is written to help you navigate through the adventure that is required to achieve such goals.

From here...

Ultimately, whether you are a classroom teacher or a leader of literacy, I wanted to create a resource that could be read quickly but meaningfully, and allow teachers and leaders of any subject to apply new understanding directly into their school context. I wanted to create a resource that could be discussed in teams and referred to alongside curriculum development, or as a guide to support specific students who aren't responding to current teaching and learning processes. I wanted to create a resource that could bridge the gap between research and the classroom, while helping secondary teachers recognise that literacy doesn't have to be scary or overwhelming, but is a powerful tool to unlock student potential, engagement and confidence.

I genuinely hope I have achieved some of these goals in bringing this text together and I optimistically look forward to hearing about the successes you have created after applying and experimenting with the information and advice in these pages.

Just remember: literacy is for life.

> **We never stop learning and growing through literacy and, as such, literacy will always be a priority in your teaching and learning – no matter the subject, year level, school or context.**

I want you to lean into this book for support. Highlight key elements you connect with and want to experiment with; download resources to engage your students or staff in the process; keep the WHY and the HOW as priorities in the classroom and in staff workshops; and reach out to me personally if you have questions beyond the pages of this book that I might be able to answer for you.

And if just a glimmer of my passion and love for literacy can rub off on you along the way… I suspect the world will be all the better for it.

Yours in all things literacy,

Hayley

Chapter 1
Why every teacher is a literacy teacher

Key chapter concept: *Literacy, holistically, is consistent – but every subject engages with its own literacy demands. Whether it is a reading, writing, speaking or listening demand, it is up to each individual teacher to teach and support their own subject-specific literacy and collectively build student efficacy to transfer and ultimately improve their literacy skills.*

Defining literacy

There are conflicting opinions and discussions that permeate a school regarding the teaching, learning and importance of literacy, as well as where the responsibility of supporting literacy might fall. So, what exactly are people referring to when they are talking about literacy, particularly in a secondary education context?

At its most basic level, **literacy** is "the ability to read and write" (Oxford English Dictionary), although this definition doesn't seem to highlight the complexities surrounding the concept of literacy in an educational setting. The Australian Curriculum, Assessment and Reporting Authority (ACARA) attempts to clarify the concept in the Australian Curriculum by defining literacy as involving:

> *"...students listening to, reading, viewing, speaking, writing and creating oral, print, visual and digital texts and using and modifying language for different purposes"* (ACARA, n.d.).

The Australian Curriculum classifies literacy as a "general capability", highlighting the importance of these skills to be taught in all subjects and year levels across the curriculum. Merga (2023) extends upon this perspective by emphasising "the importance of individual literacy in the contemporary world" and the necessity for young people to have "strong literacy skills in order to thrive in school and beyond".

But literacy, as a concept, and particularly in an education context, seems to go even further. Literacy is further defined as being a "competence or knowledge in a particular area" (Oxford English Dictionary). With this perspective, Lynch (2009) highlights 13 different types of literacies to consider in the contemporary world, each with their own vocabulary, structures and language features being used for specific effect. This classification, though, can be extended even further, as seen in Figure 1.0.

Figure 1.0: Literacy as a competence and knowledge of a specific area

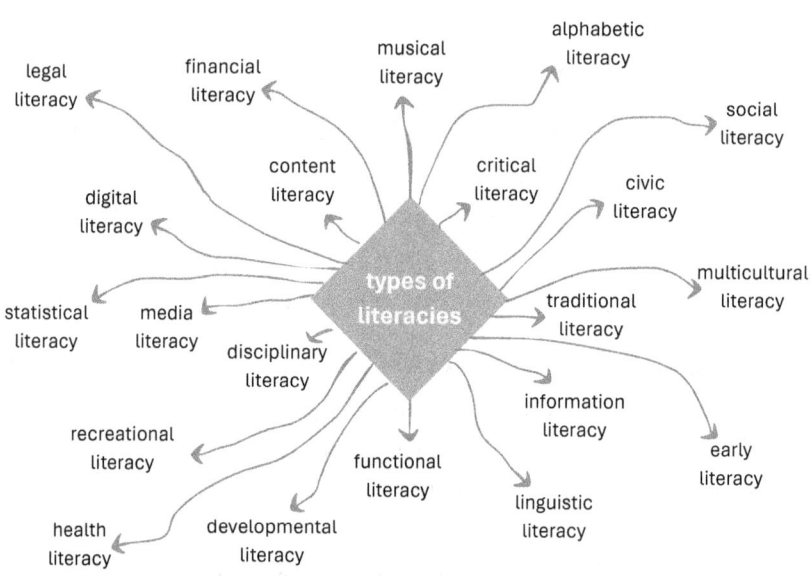

While literacy can be categorised in numerous ways, the foundation of each category begins with the essential reading, writing, speaking

and listening required to understand and communicate effectively – no matter the topic, text type, purpose or audience.

It is this communicative nature of literacy that heightens its importance and priority as a skill across a school. Due to its importance in academia and life more generally, literacy "is closely measured at individual, state, national and international levels to report on student achievement as well as to determine literacy performance and the meeting of accountabilities" (Merga, 2023). While these formalised measurements can be seen as bureaucratic or administrative attempts at accountability, their intention stems from ensuring the importance of literacy is prioritised at every level of formal education settings.

But understanding what literacy as a concept means requires teachers to extend beyond simple classifications of whether a student can read and write. These language modes are made up of several subskills, as seen in Table 1.0.

Table 1.0: Comparing the subskills of reading and writing

Reading skills	Writing skills
• phonological awareness • decoding • orthographic mapping • background knowledge (content, purpose and audience) • vocabulary • language structures (grammar) • verbal reasoning (inference and interpretation) • literacy knowledge (text types, forms, structures and features)	• phonological awareness • spelling • handwriting and typing • punctuation • background knowledge (content, purpose and audience) • vocabulary • language structures (grammar) • critical thinking (the writing process) • literacy knowledge (text types, forms, structures and features)

While primary teachers need to have the understanding and skills to teach each of these elements from a foundational point, secondary teachers face a relatively more difficult task. Secondary teachers are required:

- to teach subject-specific content and skills
- while recognising what specific reading or writing skill a student might be struggling with
- then scaffold the different reading or writing demands required in the subject to support these areas of confusion specifically
- which is likely to be different for individual students in their class
- while acknowledging that some students won't need this support at all, but rather will need to be challenged and extended.

Add to this, the alternative approaches that are recommended depending on whether a student:

- has a learning or language disorder
- is classified as English as a Second Language (EAL/EALD)
- has experienced disrupted or minimal learning in their own language
- has a physical disability that impacts their learning
- has experience of any other number of competing factors that shift the expectations of the teaching required within a class.

Suddenly, defining what literacy means and, even more so, how to possibly support and develop literacy in the increasingly complex secondary context, can seem significantly confusing, overwhelming or even insurmountable. It is important that teachers, therefore, recognise their own knowledge, experience and skills, and relish the opportunity to be in the position of a learner as they attempt to synthesise all these pieces into something that can tangibly have an impact in their classes.

Ultimately, the building of student literacy skills is a core goal of education systems because it has *the single greatest impact* on the outcomes a school can produce and the opportunities available for students post-Year 12 (Spichtig et al., 2022). Therefore, investing precious energy into building teacher understanding and capacity around literacy can only have positive outcomes for everyone across a school.

> **QUESTIONS TO CONNECT**
> - What does literacy currently mean to you, in the context of the subject/s and students you teach?
> - Which elements of teaching and supporting the literacy demands of your subject/s do you feel most confident with?
> - Which literacy skills do you find most difficult to support and develop with your students?

Literacy beyond English

The problem with literacy, as Didau (2020) states, is "a lot of literacy teaching is done unthinkingly". Literacy is simply how we communicate – either with the spoken or written word – hence, focusing on something so ingrained in day-to-day existence seems almost superfluous to the content and skills teachers are attempting to develop within their students. Rather, Didau proposes to stop thinking about embedding or adding literacy as a separate entity into lessons and rather consider it as "just plain old teaching and learning... of language". In this way, literacy shouldn't be an add-on or optional extra; instead, it should be "absolutely fundamental to every teacher's approach to pedagogy".

> *"Teaching pupils to read, write and communicate is not something special that you need to do on top of your job. It is your job!" (Didau, 2020)*

Literacy, as a whole-school responsibility, "arguably made its biggest jump towards becoming an expectation in 2014" (Merga, 2023);

however, the critical challenge for schools is to ensure literacy isn't dismissed as a passing trend or token initiative to be checked off as completed. Instead, literacy should remain embedded in classroom pedagogy across all year levels as a fundamental and integral element of teaching and learning.

The shift in thinking about literacy in the secondary context then turns to why English as a subject cannot be the place to teach the skills students need to develop and extend their literacy skills. Looking at the Australian Curriculum, the English standards specifically focus on teaching and developing the reading, writing, speaking and listening skills of every student. Additionally, English is often given more time and priority in school timetables and is often the only compulsory subject through to senior years.

If students are specifically focusing on literacy skills in their English subject, and the subject has the time and priority to do so, why does literacy then fall to *every* teacher to support, teach, provide feedback upon and prioritise?

The concept comes from the fact that while vocabulary, reading and writing skills are essentially the same no matter the unit, each subject requires a specific vocabulary for their content. Teachers require their students to read specific text types and to write in specific ways that make their subject unique. Therefore, teachers need to understand what the specific literacy requirements for their subject are and how to help their students navigate the specificity and expectations of these directly. The English teacher cannot be expected to teach the language or text structures and features of a Science report, a History source analysis or a Food Technology recipe. And it is doubtful that any Science, History or Food Technology teachers would want them to do so!

Add to this reality – there is simply not enough time. With hundreds of thousands of words in the English language, hundreds of different text types and forms, and the increasing complexity of our spelling, punctuation and **syntactic system** (sentence structure and word order) alongside increasing academic registers, a single teacher cannot hope to teach everything (no matter how amazing the English teachers are!). With so many different text purposes, audiences, structures and contexts in which schools ask students to speak, read and write, no subject – no matter how detailed or specific – can ever hope to teach them all.

> **Teachers need to realise the greatest power they have comes from their collective power to teach an individual student across different classes throughout the day.**

By considering and connecting the differences (and similarities) regarding literacy skills across different subjects, a school *can* find the time for multiple exposures of different words and strategies. They can consolidate and build retrieval practices* across a timetable as well as promote and maximise transferability of language and skills between subjects (and into the outside world).

And this is where powerful literacy reform can begin to take place.

QUESTIONS TO CONNECT

- How much of the reading and writing you ask of your students do you think is unique to your subject?
- What do you currently know about the reading and writing expectations in subjects outside the ones you teach?
- When and how do you help students transfer skills and knowledge from other subjects into your own?

---

* **Retrieval practices** are any strategy that involves recalling information without looking it up. These activities enhance long-term memory and help students internalise knowledge so they can access and apply it later. See *Check for Understanding* (page 83) for some specific retrieval practice activities.

Understanding different literacy demands

If we can accept that literacy, as a wider set of skills, is critical for students to find success in every subject – because it is the way students can access, understand, apply and show their understanding in that subject – then the next step is to recognise the similarities and differences of what literacy looks like in each subject.

The concept of **Subject-Specific Literacy** considers the specialised vocabulary and specific text types and forms for different audiences and purposes that each individual subject explores and applies. While the holistic principles of literacy as a language remain consistent, there are great variations in the expected vocabulary, expression, depth and qualities – not only across subjects, but even between different units within the same subject.

> **Whenever a teacher asks a student to read or write something in their class, they are placing a literacy demand upon that student.**

Whether that literacy demand is an instruction on the board to action, a class page to navigate, an email to decipher and reply to or something more significant such as an extended project, students will each come to this demand with different understandings, skills, experiences and motivations. As such, each demand will vary in its innate complexity, but individual students will find the same demand being more or less complex depending on what they bring to the text.

Figure 1.1 highlights some of the key elements that impact the complexity of a reading or writing demand. It is interesting to note the elements the text brings, versus what a student brings, that cause the text to be more or less complex for an individual.

Figure 1.1: Elements impacting text complexity

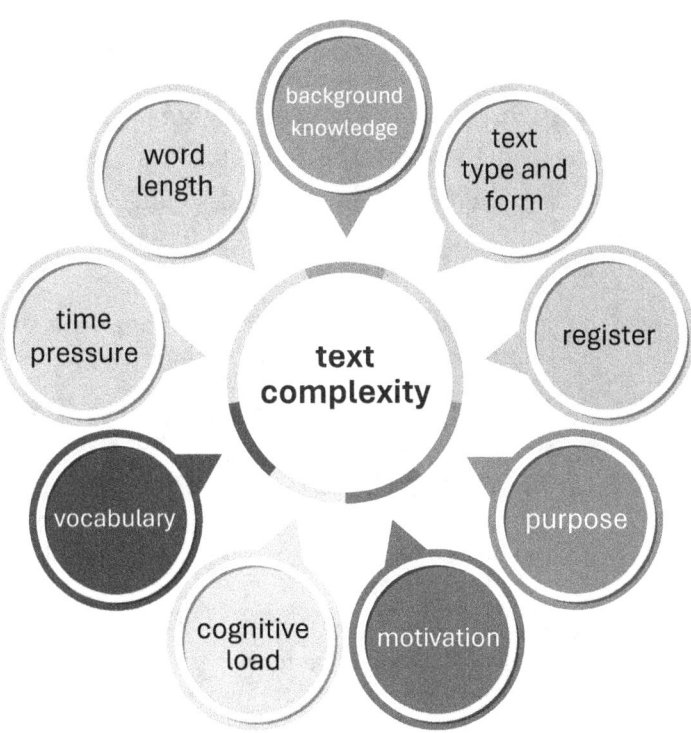

You can download a colour copy the *Text Complexity Variables* graphic in the appendices on page 195.

By acknowledging the potential complexity of the demand alongside the individual skills and knowledge students bring to the task, teachers can focus on teaching the content while understanding how to support and extend the construction of the task across the class.

Recognising the literacy demands of individual subjects highlights the subject-specific literacy across a school and the opportunities for collaboration and transference as well as the need for specialised, explicit teaching.

Table 1.1 identifies some of the potential vocabulary, reading and writing demands a student might encounter in a range of key subjects. It is interesting to identify the number of *different* text forms and terminology students might engage with and the importance for teachers to be experts in teaching their subject-specific demands.

Equally as interesting, however, is how many *similar* demands cross between subjects and therefore the opportunities these present to promote the transferability of common and significant understandings and skills.

Table 1.1: Potential vocabulary, reading and writing demands in subjects across secondary school

Subject	Vocabulary demands	Reading demands	Writing demands
Drama	theatre, performance and genre-specific terms expressive, evaluative, reflective, informative and analytical vocabulary	scripts monologues reviews/critics performance theory	structured questions research reports character analyses script writing
Food Technology	culinary and food science terms descriptive and sensory language procedural, evaluative and analytical vocabulary	recipes articles guidelines food industry reports safety regulations	recipes evaluations analytical reports research inquiries
Biology	scientific and anatomical terms precise and objective language informative, analytical and comparative vocabulary	articles/case studies laboratory reports scientific journals textbooks/ reference books	logbooks and reports scientific posters case study analyses structured questions

Subject	Vocabulary demands	Reading demands	Writing demands
Physical Education	anatomical/physiological terms performance and psychological language procedural, informative and reflective vocabulary	case studies/articles health guidelines textbooks/reference books training programs	fitness assessments training plans case study analyses reflective folios
Geography	geospatial, socioeconomic and environmental terms informative, evaluative and analytical vocabulary	climate reports sustainability policies articles/case studies textbooks and maps	survey questions fieldwork reports case study analyses annotated maps
Maths	numerical, algebraic and statistical terms logical and conceptual language descriptive, comparative and analytical vocabulary	worded problems mathematical proofs statistical reports financial modelling texts	summary notes learning logs problem-solving explanations

You can download a blank copy of a *Literacy Demands* table from the appendices on page 195 to compare the common and subject-specific demands across your school.

QUESTIONS TO CONNECT

- What specific vocabulary, reading and writing demands do you currently explore and ask students to use and create in your subjects?
- How complex are these demands for the different students in your class?
- Which of these demands falls solely to you as a subject-specific teacher to explicitly teach, and which are also being taught in other subjects?

Oral literacy: speaking and listening skills

It is important to pause here and acknowledge that literacy is more than simply reading and writing – it also encompasses the skills required to speak and listen effectively. These concepts are often marginalised in the curriculum, but as Didau (2020) argues, "It's impossible to fully separate the pedagogical process of using talk to teach and teaching talk." He explains how teachers model speaking and listening skills every time they speak and listen in class, whether they are purposefully modelling or not. As such, he argues that teachers "need to consciously model speech which moves away from everyday language and towards the academic language pupils need to access [their] subjects". This is reinforced by Alexander's (2012) large-scale study that proves "the quality of talk within classrooms raises standards".

Improving students' ability to speak and listen does far more than simply improve their **comprehension** (to understand and make meaning) or their communication skills. Explicitly focusing on talk in the classroom is a key strategy to improve both reading and writing. This is because talk is cognitive: "the way we speak changes the way we think" and "if we can say it, we can write it" (Didau, 2020).

As literacy skills, speaking and listening shouldn't be ignored, but rather, teachers need to understand the different levels of complexity these skills bring, in comparison to reading and writing. Table 1.2 highlights the significantly different processes and skills **oral literacy** requires in comparison to reading and writing.

Table 1.2: Comparing the processes involved in speaking and listening, and in reading and writing

	Speaking and listening	**Reading and writing**
Mode of communication	**Oral** – real-time interaction, using tone and non-verbal cues	**Written** – interaction happens in a different time and space, using grammar and formatting cues
Cognitive processing	**Spontaneous** – requiring quick thinking and response	**Deliberate** – allowing time for reflection and revision
Feedback	**Immediate** – adjustments and questions can be made and answered in real time	**Delayed** – revision and editing are used to predict questions and minimise confusions
Memory and retention	**Temporary** – relying on auditory and working memory	**Permanent** – allowing for future reference and deeper analysis

It is important for teachers to recognise that the cognitive demands and thought processes required for speaking and listening differ significantly from those involved in reading and writing. This is because speaking is a biological primary skill that humans are generally able to learn naturally without explicit teaching. In contrast, reading and writing are essentially cultural inventions that require explicit and systematic teaching and repetition for a person to learn and apply.

It is this fact that has ultimately influenced why this text only spends a moment considering the teaching of speaking and listening and will spend whole chapters exploring the teaching of reading and writing. However, it is still important for teachers to never assume students' level of speaking and listening skills and strategies, and to recognise the benefits of building student capacity to communicate effectively.

The following five strategies, processes and activities can be used as ways to support and explicitly develop students' speaking and listening skills in any classroom.

1. Accountable Talk

Building upon Vygotsky's learning theories, Resnick, Asterhan and Clarke (2018) explain the role of dialogue in cognitive development and highlight different strategies to explicitly teach and foster meaningful classroom discussions through *Accountable Talk*. The concept focuses on establishing clear norms for discussion and different sentence starters and strategies to guide conversations.

These include:

a. Pressing for reasoning – '*What evidence supports your idea…?*'
b. Revoicing contributions – '*So, you're saying that…?*'
c. Connecting ideas – '*So, your idea connects with the idea that…?*'
d. Encouraging elaboration – '*Can you explain what you mean by…?*'
e. Challenging assumptions – '*Is there another way you could…?*'

Students are required to justify and support their thinking and be respectful in ways that oppose or challenge another person's ideas and perspectives. After discussions, students are given time to reflect on the process and their strengths and areas for focus regarding holding meaningful discussions.

Table 1.3: *Accountable Talk* example sentence starters

Challenge	- Why do you think…? - Couldn't it also be…? - Where can I find that idea or example…? - Perhaps an alternative could be… - Can you explain…? - Why might…? - When did…? - How do you know…?
Extend	- Can you restate…? - What's another example…? - I'd like to know more about… - I can expand upon that by adding… - What difference is…? - What strategy did you use…? - When you said… what does that mean? - Can you elaborate…?
Reflect	- I wonder why/if… - I changed my mind after… - I would like to add… - If I understand this correctly, it means… - From my perspective… - This reminds me of… - One idea I have about… - Does anyone else think…?
Justify	- I think this because… - I agreed/disagreed with this after… - I was confused about… until… - I can prove this with/by… - I believe this is true due to… - This is seen when… - While some might think… actually… - This is most clearly evident by considering…

2. Socratic Circles

Also known as *Socratic Seminars* or *Fishbowls*, the process involves two groups of students physically seated in two inwardly facing circles.

Students in the inner circle discuss a text, question or topic they have had time to read and explore beforehand. They need to come to the discussion prepared with their ideas, interpretations, reasoning and evidence.

Students in the outer circle observe the inner circle discussion, taking notes on the ideas, participation, reasoning and evidence being used.

After a set amount of time (this can vary depending on the year level, number of students involved or the complexity of the topic), those in the outer circle are asked to reflect upon the observations before either switching roles or using the discussion to formulate a written response more formally.

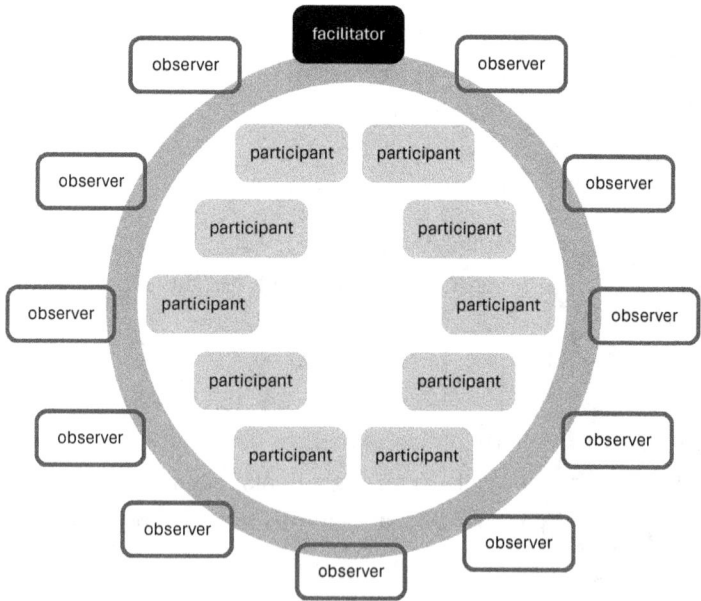

Figure 1.2: Example layout of the classroom set-up for a *Socratic Circle* discussion

3. The Third Move

Robin Alexander's Dialogic Teaching concept (2020) refers to the moment in a classroom discussion when a teacher responds to a student's contribution in a way that either extends and deepens or closes down and limits thinking.

Third Move opportunities sustain student thinking to promote more critical, engaged and purposeful discussions. They align well with the concepts explored in *Accountable Talk* (see page 26).

Third Move responses might include:

- **Probing for reasoning**
    - 'Can you explain why you think that?'
    - 'Can you give me an example that illustrates your point?'
- **Building on ideas**
    - 'How does that connect to what we discussed earlier?'
    - 'Can we apply what you've just said to a different situation?'
- **Introducing alternative perspectives**
    - 'How might someone else with a different experience see this?'
    - 'Is there another way to interpret this information?'
- **Encouraging peer interaction**
    - 'Can someone build upon what has just been said?'
    - 'Who can challenge or extend upon this idea?'
    - 'Who can then give an example of what has just been said?'

Table 1.4: Alternative *Third Move* responses for varying effect

1. Teacher	What are the two types of power?			
2. Student	Soft and hard power.			
3. Teacher	Great. That is correct. Soft and hard power.	Yes, soft power co-opts or attracts, while hard power threatens or coerces.	That is correct. Can you give me an example of each?	And what is the difference between them?
Impact of the *Third Move*	**Feedback** closes thinking down	**Clarification** does the thinking for the student	**Elaboration** deepens thinking	**Extension** extends thinking

4. Think-Aloud

A cognitive strategy based on Wilhelm Wundt's introspection techniques in psychology, a *Think-Aloud* is used to make thought processes visible by verbalising them as a person is working through a task.

It can be used as an effective modelling strategy for the teacher to help explain the process of a task, but it can also be encouraged as a way for students to reflect on their own thinking processes and consider the opportunities they need to recognise when they aren't thinking, questioning or being metacognitively active while attempting complex tasks.

Instructions:

- Clarify the purpose: decide what the priority of learning is.
- Select the text or task: choose a short, rich excerpt or task that lends itself to visible reasoning.
- Plan your script: outline key moves to model and what to emphasise. Anticipate questions, misconceptions and decisions.
- Model with precision: speak slowly and clearly, using expressive intonation and gestures if helpful. Focus on your verbs, for example, 'I notice…', 'I wonder…' and 'I'm choosing…', as well as your time markers: 'now', 'next', 'and then' and 'before that'.
- Invite student reflection: question what they noticed and what strategies they could try.
- Acknowledge what thinking process students go through when they are working independently. Do they ask themselves questions along the way? How might this help?

---

5. Active Listening

Another cognitive approach (introduced in 1957 by Rogers and Farson) is a communication technique that involves explicitly teaching students the importance of concentrating, understanding, responding and remembering what someone has said when speaking.

In contrast to *Passive Listening*, *Active Listening* requires engagement, empathy and intentional focus using both verbal and non-verbal cues. Generally, people only remember 20–50% of what they hear, depending on how actively they listen. Explicitly teaching the skills and benefits of *Active Listening* develops beneficial classroom and life skills.

The key techniques of *Active Listening* include:

a. **Paying full attention:** We are often thinking about what to say next – or something different altogether – rather than listening to what a person is saying. Listening is about focusing not just on the words being spoken, but also on the speaker's tone, expression and body language.

b. **Showing listening:** Sometimes eye contact can feel forced or threatening, but often it is the best way to show a person you are listening. Other ways you can show you are listening are through your facial expressions, nodding, gestures and body language.

c. **Providing feedback:** Nodding is a form of non-verbal feedback, but good listeners will be able to ask appropriate questions, paraphrase or reflect upon what the speaker has said, and give insights or connections (this is where *Accountable Talk* comes into play).

d. **Deferring judgement:** *Active Listening* requires waiting until the speaker has finished before responding. Listening requires an open mind and waiting for all the information before deciding how to respond. Often, people only listen to the first few things someone says and then they switch off. *Active Listening* means staying focused and using the information.

e. **Responding appropriately:** Different situations will require different responses after listening. As part of an audience, listening to a speech requires a specific type of *Active Listening* and response, rather than having a conversation with a friend. So, too, does listening to instructions compared to being an active listener and participant in a group project.

QUESTIONS TO CONNECT

- How do you explicitly teach, support and model speaking and listening skills?
- What aspect of speaking and listening do your students find most difficult?
- What language and strategies around speaking and listening does your school use that you could transfer and extend upon in your classes?

Bringing everything together

Once it is understood that literacy must be a whole-school priority because of the collective power across each subject, and how it is up to the individual teacher to teach and support the subject-specific literacy of their subject, the final (rather large) step is to ensure every teacher understands *how* to explicitly teach, scaffold, consolidate, transfer and extend literacy skills within their classes.

Teachers simply cannot teach what they do not know or understand, but once they are able to recognise the:

- importance of literacy for any student to find success
- specific literacy demands of the subject/s and year level/s they teach
- importance of every teacher prioritising and explicitly teaching the literacy demands within their subject
- opportunities available to transfer and consolidate literacy across subjects…

…then schools have a genuine ability to truly begin to transform the lives of the students under their care and guidance – and that is pretty exciting.

Connect: from page to practice

In your faculty or subject teams:

1. Discuss and decide what literacy means and looks like in the context of your subject.

2. Discuss the impact literacy has upon the students in your subject. What priority does it have overall?

3. Rate the top literacy-specific skills students find most difficult to master or extend in your subject.

4. Identify the language and approaches your team currently uses to support literacy and which skills they find most difficult to teach, support and extend.

Why every teacher is a literacy teacher... in summary

What is literacy?
Literacy, as a concept, refers to the skills a person needs to read, write, speak and listen effectively enough to understand and communicate.

It's how we learn...
In a school context, literacy is the way a student understands content (listening and reading) and shows this understanding (speaking and writing).

In every subject...
Due to the specialised vocabulary, reading and writing demands in each subject, literacy must be considered a vital teaching and learning focus, rather than an addition, in every classroom.

Working together
An individual teacher doesn't have the time or capacity to consolidate and support the literacy development for students alone, but by **every** teacher working **collaboratively**, the transferability of literacy skills can be prioritised and maximised.

Speaking and listening
The value and importance of explicitly teaching and modelling speaking and listening skills shouldn't be ignored but simply balanced against the complexity of reading and writing.

Key priorities
For teachers to:
- identify and understand the literacy demands of their subject
- have a variety of ways to prioritise, scaffold and transfer the literacy demands in every class

Teaching through literacy
Understanding the vocabulary, reading and writing demands in any classroom, or for any unit of work, will allow teachers to focus on the scaffolding and explicit teaching required for their students to find success. This is not about **adding** to their teaching, or deprioritising the content and skills of their subject, but rather understanding how to teach the skills and knowledge of their subject **THROUGH** literacy.

Connecting Whole-School Literacy in the Secondary Context

Chapter 2
Connecting vocabulary

Key chapter concept: *Teaching vocabulary requires more than simply providing the definitions of the technical words in a unit. Students also require access to the academically precise words to discuss the technical terms taught. To convert a new word to their active vocabulary, students need to understand the implied or emotional meaning of the word, as well as be able to pronounce, spell and change the word, so they can use it effectively when speaking and writing.*

The importance of teaching and learning vocabulary

While it might seem somewhat obvious to propose that teaching and learning vocabulary is important in any classroom, the significance and impact of vocabulary reaches into almost every facet of a student's life. "Vocabulary is a strong predictor of reading comprehension and fluency" (Scali, 2023) and "vocabulary knowledge accounts for 26% of variance in writing performance" (Kiliç, 2019). These correlations, between vocabulary and reading and writing, then extend well into high school (Beck et al., 2013), exacerbating the literacy gap among cohorts.

The Oxford Language Report (Bolton, 2020) builds upon this concept by highlighting how a limited vocabulary not only affects a child's potential academic success, but "it can also affect their behaviour, their self-esteem and ultimately their life chances". The report reveals how 92% of teachers believe the vocabulary gap has become worse since the Covid-19 closures, and that the "transition between primary and secondary is particularly problematic".

"By Year 9, the spread of vocabulary attainment (based on trends in NAPLAN) spans eight years," say Goss and Sonnemann (2016). This diversity then poses a "substantial challenge for teachers in mainstream classes seeking to provide learning experiences that meet the skills and abilities of all their students" (Walker & Bayetto, 2021). Interestingly, Albright, Knezevic and Farrell (2013) postulate the "most common factor influencing curriculum implementation" for Australian secondary teachers is the "range of student vocabulary" within their class.

This body of research into the impact of vocabulary development in the secondary environment shows how vocabulary impacts not only a student's *understanding* of concepts and knowledge, but also their ability to *read and comprehend* texts, and to *articulate their understanding* when writing for different contexts and purposes.

Focusing on building vocabulary will support the development of both reading and writing, and therefore a student's understanding and application of any knowledge explicitly taught.

Barriers to developing vocabulary in the secondary context, however, are seen in the study of Swanborn and de Glopper (1999), who found 5th- to 11th-grade students have only a 15% probability of learning a new word from an incidental encounter. This reveals how, although text exposure does correlate with learning words, it is not enough for students to simply be exposed to words in order to learn them.

Building vocabulary requires explicit and purposeful teaching across the secondary curriculum.

Alex Quigley, in his text *Closing the Vocabulary Gap* (2018), highlights the necessity of training teachers to become more knowledgeable and confident in explicit vocabulary teaching as the "number one step to close the vocabulary gap". The first action to this vital understanding, therefore, begins with understanding *how* a person builds vocabulary in the first place.

> **QUESTIONS TO CONNECT**
>
> - What vocabulary barriers do the students in your class struggle with the most?
> - Where do your students access and acquire the words they currently use when speaking and writing?
> - How do you currently teach vocabulary, and how effective do you find this to be?

Learning new words

The way an individual learns the spoken and written components of any language – as a child or an adult learning a second language – has long been explored in neuroscience. While language acquisition is confidently attributed to the left side of the brain, more current research also highlights the complex relationship with the right side of the brain. Here, more of the inferential language functions occur, including the ability to comprehend metaphors and patterns of intonation.

Teachers do not necessarily need to know the exact scientific terminology and theory associated with language development, but they do need to understand how a student learns new words (and how they don't!) to maximise the opportunities they have in the classroom.

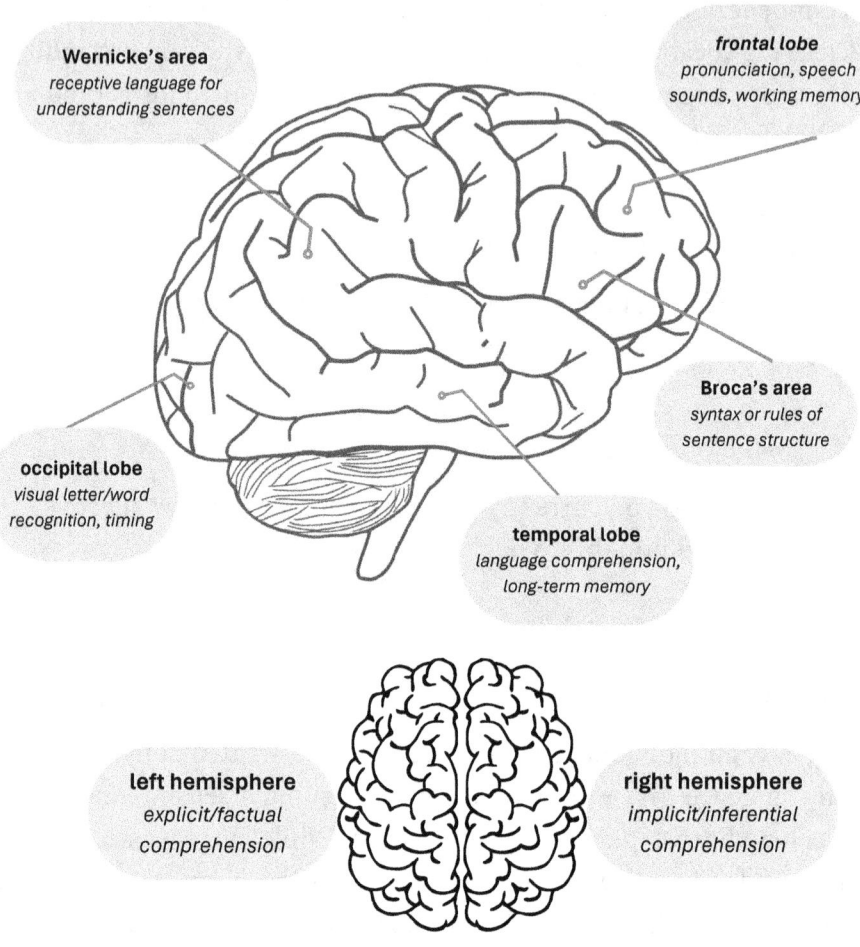

Figure 2.0: Brain areas related to the skill of comprehension and reading

The specific skills required for a person to **decode** (read a new word) and **encode** (spell a new word) are essentially the same. This makes it even more important for students to explicitly be taught these skills. A problem many secondary teachers face, however, is that most of these skills 'should' have been taught in primary school, and yet for numerous reasons, many students are arriving in secondary school with distinct and varied gaps in these skills. This means that whole-class approaches to these foundational skills are often not effective ways to approach the vocabulary gap found in so many secondary classrooms.

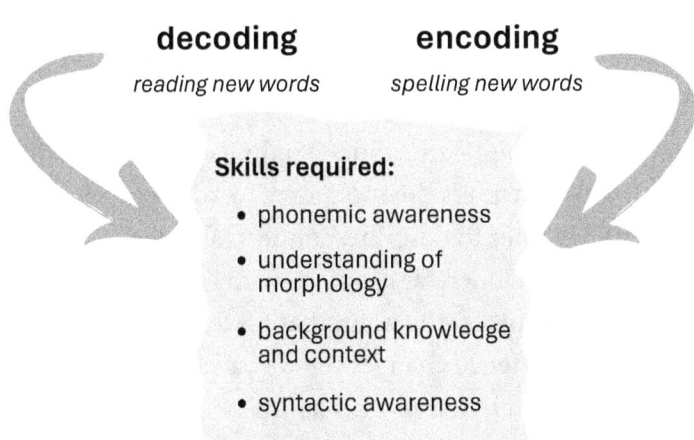

Figure 2.1: The similar skills required to decode and encode unfamiliar words

To decode or encode new words, students require:

- **Phonemic awareness** – the ability to connect the letters and combinations of letters with the sounds they can represent. While the strategy of 'sounding out' a word is not always the best or strongest strategy, it is the most logical starting point for any person attempting to decode or encode a word for the first time. *Note: if a student is mispronouncing a word, they are much more likely to spell the word incorrectly.*

- **Morphological awareness** – the ability to connect the meaningful parts of a word with the overall meaning of the word. Morphological awareness should extend into and throughout secondary school as students explore more sophisticated prefixes (such as: infra-, mono-, omni-) and suffixes (such as: -ify, -ism, -acy) and as a highly relevant and effective way to introduce new technical language being taught across subjects.

- **Background knowledge and context** – the understanding of the text type, audience and purpose of the text, and therefore the intentions of the word being used. This becomes increasingly relevant as more sophisticated and academic texts are explored and written (such as articles, case studies, research papers). Understanding text structures and features allows students to connect specific vocabulary with voice and audience.

- **Syntactic awareness** – the understanding of the **syntactic system***. This considers the function a word is playing in a sentence; whether to describe, connect, show tense or importance, etc. Understanding if a word is describing another word or is the **subject** (the noun that performs the action of the verb) of a sentence changes the way a student can connect with what the unfamiliar term is *doing*.

A person's ability to retrieve a word is incredible, but not necessarily efficient, which is why the tip-of-the-tongue phenomenon is so common! In one study, where researchers mapped the time course of word retrieval, they found participants, on average, selected words within 200 milliseconds (Castro, 2023).

But to decode a word, de Zubicaray (2023) highlights how the brain must go through several stages of processing:

1. Identifying the intended meaning
2. Selecting the right word from the **mental lexicon** (a mental dictionary of the speaker's vocabulary)
3. Retrieving its sound pattern
4. Executing the movements of the speech organs for articulating (if reading aloud).

---

* **Syntatic system:** the word choice and rules that determine how those words can be ordered in sentences and how punctuation can be used to support meaning.

The process of **orthographic mapping** (the way words are stored in the long-term memory) was first documented by Linnea Ehri in the 1970s and explains the process our brains go through when committing a word to memory so it can be retrieved automatically.

> *"Orthographic mapping involves the formation of letter-sound connections to bond the spellings, pronunciations, and meanings of specific words in memory. It explains how children learn to read words by sight, to spell words from memory, and to acquire vocabulary words from print"* (Ehri, 2014).

The mapping process to encode vocabulary is similar to the process for reading a word, but for an individual to write a word they have to:

1. Identify the meaning they are trying to express.
2. Select the right word from their mental lexicon.
3. Retrieve the alphabetic representations (letters) at the same time as execute accurate spelling patterns.
4. Execute the movement of the hand, arms and stabilising body to replicate each letter in legible ways onto paper.
5. Hold on to the meaning of the overall sentence while processing each word individually.

The heightened complexity of writing, considering the **cognitive load** (the brain's working capacity during learning) required to write, becomes immediately apparent in the recall of words when compared with speaking or reading.

> **This complexity is why student writing is often significantly less sophisticated, accurate or precise than a student's spoken comprehension of a concept or text: their brain must work that much harder!**

To some extent, learners' language contexts define the specific skills they need to develop and the opportunities they have to do so (Knoph et al., 2024). Yet, while a school cannot control the communication, reading or exposure to vocabulary that occur before a student enters Year 7, teachers *can* control the teaching and learning of vocabulary conducted and scaffolded within the school environment. This, therefore, should be the focus for any classroom teacher – to provide students with the gift to understand and be understood.

> **QUESTIONS TO CONNECT**
> - How does understanding the similarities and differences between decoding and encoding unfamiliar words help you teach vocabulary more effectively in your classes?
> - What gaps in the skills required to decode and encode have you most commonly witnessed in your students struggling with reading and/or writing?

Active and passive vocabulary

Oftentimes, when teachers are discussing teaching or building student vocabulary, the focus is on whether the student understands the *meaning* of the word. This understanding is obviously critical for a student to comprehend and use the word accurately, but this limited focus doesn't take into consideration the difference between a student's active and passive vocabulary.

When a person can read or hear a word and understand its meaning, they are using their **passive vocabulary**. When they are using words in their writing or speaking, they are drawing from their **active vocabulary**.

Eide (2012) considers the average passive (or receptive) vocabulary for an adult is around 40,000 to 60,000 words (a well-educated adult mastering up to 200,000), while the average active (or productive) vocabulary is only between 5,000 and 7,000 (for a native speaker without a higher education), and up to 20,000 to 40,000 (for a native speaker with a higher education).

Figure 2.2: Active and passive vocabulary

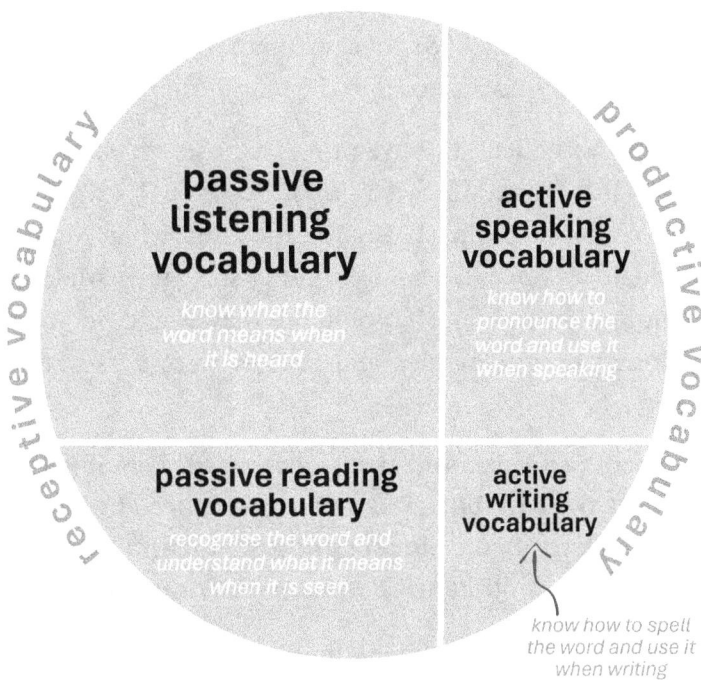

The impact of this vocabulary discrepancy is most markedly seen when assessing students' comprehension and understanding of content. They often demonstrate understanding when reading and listening but cannot articulate this understanding (particularly in sophisticated ways) when speaking or writing. It's not necessarily because they don't understand, but rather they don't have the active vocabulary to draw from to articulate their understanding.

But how many times does an individual have to hear, read, say or write a word for it to be considered part of their vocabulary? Data around the number of exposures a person might require before a word is fully understood varies quite drastically. Ehri (2014) suggests that as an individual encounters a word, it moves through **partial mapping** (the early stages of orthographic mapping) after three to four exposures and **full orthographic mapping** (having a word stored in the long-term memory) after *at least 12–15 exposures*. Marzano (2005) proposed 15 times; Share (2008) considered 10–20; while Miller and Gildea (1987) pushed that to 30–50 exposures before orthographic mapping occurred in the long-term memory.

For a struggling student, however, these exposures generally need to increase by at least two to three times. Bosse et al. (2007) consider a dyslexic reader might need 40–60 exposures, while Montgomery, Ilk and Moats (2012) extend this, arguing struggling students could require more than *200 repetitions* before they would no longer need to consciously decode a word and reliably have it as part of their mental lexicon.

The process to learn and store new words remains the same, but the number of exposures required before these words can be subconsciously understood and actively drawn varies significantly for each individual in a class.

The ultimate goal for teachers should be around building a student's active vocabulary and extending the words they feel confident and comfortable to use when speaking and writing about the content of any particular subject. Focusing on *using* rather than simply *knowing* new words shifts the way teachers experiment with and engage students in new terminology as it presents itself in the classroom.

QUESTIONS TO CONNECT

- If a student can understand significantly more of the content you teach than they can express or articulate, how can you accurately assess their understanding?
- Where and how can you purposefully maximise the exposures and retrieval practice of vocabulary in your classes to promote and increase a student's active vocabulary?

Classifying vocabulary

With between 170,000 and 2 million words in the English language (depending on what statistic one chooses to believe), schools cannot hope to explicitly teach every word in the dictionary. Research estimates students will generally acquire 2,000–5,000 new words every year during secondary school. Graves (2006) breaks this down further, explaining how around 500–1,000 of these words are explicitly taught and promoted as being actively used, while the rest are receptive (passive) vocabulary built through the academic and extended reading required throughout senior year levels. This statistic highlights not only the importance of explicit vocabulary instruction, but also how the vocabulary gap can widen between those students who are actively reading beyond the minimum classroom expectations and their less academically motivated peers, or between students at schools requiring drastically different reading experiences and expectations.

As teachers, it can be useful to classify words to help process which words to focus on and how best to approach the vocabulary development for specific students. While schools want to expose students to the greatest number of words possible, they have to be realistic about how many words teachers can explicitly (or even incidentally) teach. Considering classifications of words allows teachers to focus on the point of greatest impact and potentially balance this across the school and year levels.

The concept of classifying vocabulary into 'tiers' was introduced by Beck, McKeown and Kucan in 2013. The **Three Tiers of Vocabulary** model (as seen in Figure 2.3) exposes the potential disparity of time dedicated to the subject-specific (technical: tier 3) vocabulary of a unit, while assumptions are made that students have the academic (tier 2) vocabulary to respond in sophisticated and formal ways. Understanding these classifications can help teachers recognise the need to balance their teaching across the tiers and support the transference of tier 2 words across units, year levels and subjects.

Figure 2.3: The Three Tiers of Vocabulary

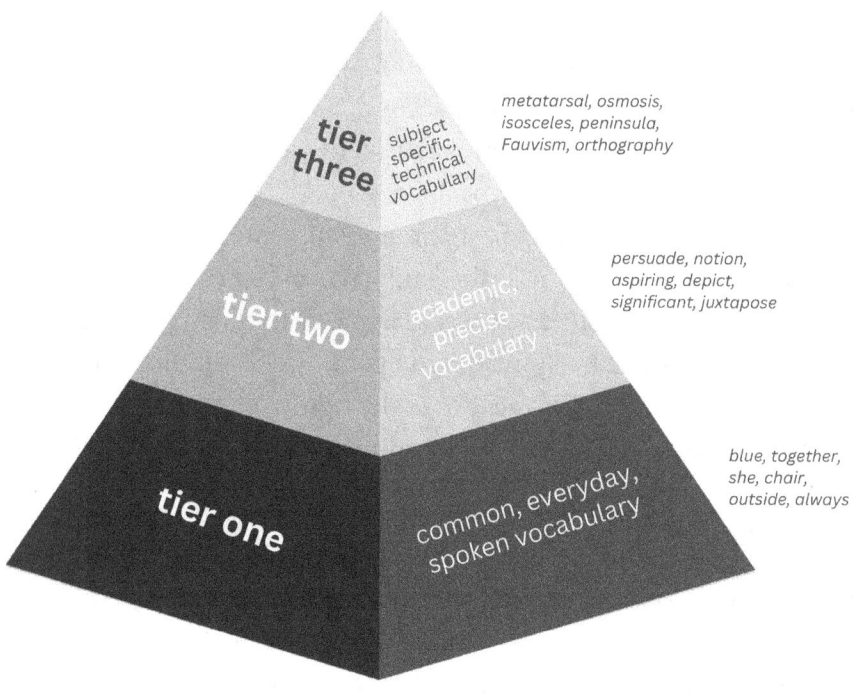

Tier 1 consists of everyday, common words individuals generally learn through spoken communication. These words rarely require explicit teaching and are words students heavily draw from to articulate their understanding. Tier 1 words are commonly being overused when students 'write the way they speak'. While these words might make up most of a student's active vocabulary, this does not mean there won't potentially be issues with the spelling or manipulation of these words when writing.

Tier 2 consists of academic, specific vocabulary. These words are used across subjects and units, and often are the descriptive words used to make a text more sophisticated and precise. Tier 2 vocabulary often includes tier 1 words that can be used as synonyms but hold stronger connotations and more precise meanings than these other simpler terms. These words are less likely to be explicitly taught as they are numerous and not subject-specific; however, they are some of the most powerful tools students can have when building their wider and more academic expression.

A subcategory of tier 2 vocabulary contains the **command (or instructional) words** that are used in questions, tasks, topics or assessments. These are either action verbs or question words that explain what a student is specifically supposed to do to respond accurately.

Table 2.0: Common command terms used in secondary settings

analyse	annotate	apply	assess
calculate	clarify	comment	compare
consider	construct	contrast	deduce
define	demonstrate	describe	design
determine	develop	discuss	distinguish
estimate	evaluate	examine	explain
extract	extrapolate	highlight	identify
infer	interpret	investigate	justify
label	list	name	outline
persuade	predict	propose	recall
recommend	recount	show	sketch
state	suggest	summarise	synthesise

You can download a copy of *Common Command Terms* in the appendices on page 195.

Highlighting the similarities between terms (to suggest, recommend or propose are all fairly close synonyms) against significant differences (to label, explain or evaluate all require very different responses) allows students to focus on the specific *action* required in their response as confirmed within the question. By focusing on the command term and then changing just the term within a question, students not only engage with the content in different ways but consolidate their understanding of, and the impact of, these critical terms at the same time.

For example:

- Explain the differences between classical and operant conditioning.
- Outline the differences between classical and operant conditioning.
- Evaluate the differences between classical and operant conditioning.
- Discuss the differences between classical and operant conditioning.

This epitomises the concept of *using* rather than *adding* literacy into disciplinary curriculum.

Command terms are used across every subject, unit and year level, and are often explicitly explored in senior levels as assessment tasks build in importance and specificity. Confusion can occur, however, when teachers either don't use them consciously enough – for example, asking students to 'explain' when they mean 'evaluate' or 'define' – or they don't highlight the variance in meaning across subjects.

For example:

| To **analyse** in English requires the identification of key elements in a text to explore how those pieces contribute to a deeper meaning and interpretation of the text. This requires an extended and detailed written response, including numerous pieces of evidence and analytical verbs throughout. | To **analyse** in Mathematics requires the breaking down of a problem into simpler parts and the use of specific formulas and numerical moves to find answers. It results in a definitive answer, most often written as numbers and/or symbols. |

Tier 3 vocabulary is the most technical and specialised category of words. These are the words most often explicitly taught in all subjects as the key terms and content required in any unit. These words rarely have synonyms and are only used in specific units of work and contexts. Generally, these terms are taught as nouns and students are expected to use them in their assessments to show knowledge and understanding of a topic.

Overall, considering the imposing number of repetitions required for some students to orthographically map these new words into their long-term memory and move these terms into their active vocabulary, any vocabulary focus requires an entire school, in every year level and subject, to collectively maximise exposure and promote the importance and impact of building academic vocabulary.

> **Beyond the subject-specific vocabulary, suddenly a secondary goal for teachers is to consider how and when they can explicitly focus on building tier 2 vocabulary alongside the tier 3 vocabulary they are currently teaching.**

QUESTIONS TO CONNECT

- How balanced is your teaching of technical words versus academic words in your classes?
- Which academic and command terms are most often used in your subject area, and do all subject teachers have the same understanding of the expectations when using this word?
- Who is responsible for teaching these words and when does this happen?

Choosing words to teach

Determining which words will be explicitly taught, when and where, can feel like an insurmountable task for an individual teacher, let alone a whole school. Teachers need to be selective about which words they need to prioritise, which words they need to scope and sequence across a unit, subject or year level, and where they can embed vocabulary to 'incidentally' discover along the way.

Linguists and researchers have created numerous word lists to help educators target high-frequency words in different contexts. Some of the larger scale and relevant word lists include:

- **The Oxford 3000 or 5000** – a list of 3,000 (or 5,000) core words chosen based on their frequency in the Oxford English Corpus.
- **The Academic Word List (AWL)** – 570 word families pulled from Arts, Commerce, Law and Science texts and excluding the General Service List (more than 2,000 of the most frequently used words).
- **The Academic Vocabulary List (AVL)** – 500 words pulled from the most frequent words found in academic texts, whether these are included in the General Service List or not.

You can download a copy of Common Academic Words in the appendices on page 195.

While a school does not want to simply take a list of words and systematically work through embedding them into the curriculum across different subjects, these types of lists allow teachers to consider which words might have the greatest impact (if the frequency of coming across the word is going to be higher) and can help in building appropriate word banks for teachers across disciplines to consider and prioritise.

Activities like *All the Words Around* (see page 59) can help teachers notice common and relevant terms for their subject. Looking through exemplar student writing from previous years can also help highlight strong vocabulary options that can more explicitly be planned for and taught in future years. This can often be a more productive way to generate purposeful word lists for the curriculum; just remember to *embed*, rather than simply list, them within your curriculum.

All of this, however, might start seeming insurmountable.

How can a single teacher teach the gaps in vocabulary and explicitly teach enough words to build the academic vocabulary of a student, by ensuring these new terms are repeated 15, 40 or more than 200 times?!

The short answer is: the single teacher cannot, but if every teacher, across Years 7–12, plays their role in this development, then this is where the magic happens. It is just important that these teachers understand what needs to be prioritised when attempting to teach vocabulary.

> **QUESTIONS TO CONNECT**
>
> - How many new words are you planning to explicitly teach and expose your students to across a unit and within each lesson?
> - Which words would you most like your students to be using that they currently are not?

Going beyond the definition

Dale (1965) classifies vocabulary development as the Four Stages of Word Knowledge, where students identify if they:

1. have never heard of the word
2. have heard of it but don't know what it means
3. know the word has something to do with…
4. know it well and can explain it in context.

Teachers, however, need to take this concept even further if they want to transfer a word into a student's active vocabulary. They need to consider if a student also knows how to:

1. pronounce and use the word in spoken contexts
2. spell and use the word in written contexts
3. change the word to use in different contexts and ways within a sentence.

In this way, after teachers recognise *what* words need to be taught, they then need to acknowledge and understand that teaching vocabulary must be *more than simply knowing the definition*. Providing students with a list of glossary terms, or simply explaining a word's meaning if a student incidentally asks, not only minimises the exposure students have to that unfamiliar word, but it does not promote the student building this word into their *active* vocabulary.

Remember: a student needs to be able to *say* and *spell* a word for them to be able to *use* the word.

One simple technique to ensure maximum exposure and promote the application of a new word is: *Hear the word, See the word, Say the word, Write the word (HSSW)*. This simple approach can be used as part of the explicit teaching of new vocabulary, or at a moment of incidental teaching when a student asks for clarification on a word they come across.

The concept builds a framework to ensure students get to hear the word and then say it aloud so they can feel confident in its pronunciation, meaning they are more likely to use it as part of their spoken vocabulary. It also enables them to see and write the word so they can more confidently spell and apply it in their written responses. This process should only take a minute of teaching but ensures students have more than four exposures to the word as well as ways they can use it in different contexts.

Figure 2.4: The *HSSW* model

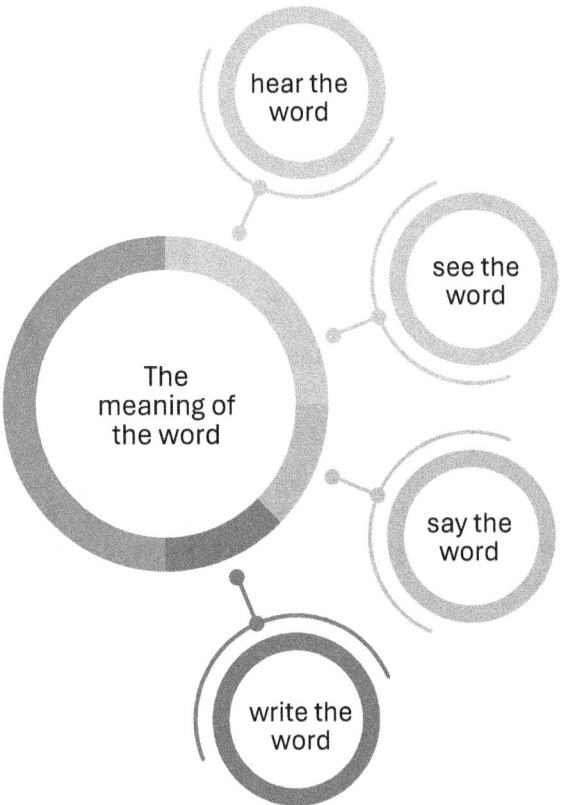

You can download a colour copy of the *HSSW* graphic in the appendices on page 195.

Classroom example

> **Teacher:** At this point I am just looking for a modicum of respect from the class...
>
> **Student:** What does 'modicum' mean?
>
> **Teacher:** Fabulous question. 'Modicum' means the smallest amount of something, so I was looking for even the smallest amount of respect, not everything, but just some. I used it as an exaggeration to highlight that the class wasn't giving me any respect at all.
>
> (writes modicum on the board while speaking)
>
> Notice 'modicum' is spelt pretty much the way it sounds but 'c-u-m' rather than 'c-o-m-e' like you might expect at the end. Can everyone please say the word 'modicum' out loud together?
>
> **Students:** Modicum.
>
> **Teacher:** Beautiful. Have a go at writing it down so you can see it in your own handwriting. Check you've spelt it correctly. And just like that you are already showing me more than a modicum of respect! So, let's get on with the class...

The key to teaching vocabulary is to purposefully plan to teach specific words – but also engage in the vocabulary of texts to more authentically build students' vocabulary. By acknowledging the *sounds* (phonology) through hearing and saying the word, *spelling* (orthography) through seeing and writing the word, and *meaning* (morphology) by not only giving the definition but acknowledging its connotation or how it is used in context, teachers can more confidently achieve the goal of students not only understanding but *applying* the word in both their speaking and writing.

An additional step to *HSSW* is to consider and explore a word's *derivations*. These are the ways a word can change the function it plays within a sentence.

For example, by changing its suffix, a person can choose to use the word '*persuade*' as:

- A <u>verb</u>: I will *persuade* you.
- A <u>noun</u>: The *persuasion* was strong.
- An <u>adverb</u>: I argued my point *persuasively*.
- An <u>adjective</u>: The *persuasive* article was life changing.

Introducing the different derivational moves that can be made with a new term means that rather than simply teaching what it means to 'critique' something, students can be extended to experiment with how they can also be 'critical', write 'critically', have 'criticism' or be a 'critic' as well. Suddenly, one word has gifted five words and a variety of uses for students to draw from wherever appropriate.

Vocabulary activities for every classroom

While purposefully planning to teach vocabulary is the first step, knowing *how* to effectively teach vocabulary will ultimately produce the greatest impact.

There are innumerable ways a teacher can explicitly teach, experiment or engage with vocabulary in their classroom. Having a variety of strategies and activities that can be used in different contexts allows teachers to best consider the specific subjects, cohorts and individual student needs from one year to another.

The following five activities can be used in any classroom and for any content in various ways depending on need, ability, set-up and time available.

1. SEA It

Students are given a word that has previously been explicitly taught and are asked to:

- **S**pell it (after the teacher has spoken it aloud).
- **E**xplain it (provide a definition of what the word means).
- **A**pply it (use the word appropriately in a sentence).

As an activity, *SEA It* works well as a **bell-ringer** or **exit slip** (initial or end of a lesson activity), activation of prior knowledge, retrieval practice or brain break activity. It is less effective and too time-consuming (and potentially disengaging) to complete a list of words in this way, but strategies such as *SEA It* allow teachers to quickly and efficiently access individual students' understanding of a single concept.

This strategy is a more effective way to formatively assess student understanding rather than simply asking the class what a concept means and getting a single student answering on behalf of the class. This also checks individual students can use the term accurately and have the language to use it in context, while maximising the exposure of the word to support the transition into their active vocabulary.

An extension to *SEA It* is to challenge students to apply the word in an academic sentence, experimenting with other precise and sophisticated words they have been exploring.

Classroom example

While teachers can choose to print and distribute slips such as Figure 2.5, the *SEA It* strategy is just as effective when using mini-whiteboards, workbooks or scraps of paper. *SEA It* responses can be left on student desks to check throughout the class or are easily peer-/self-assessed.

Figure 2.5: Example *SEA It* Ticket

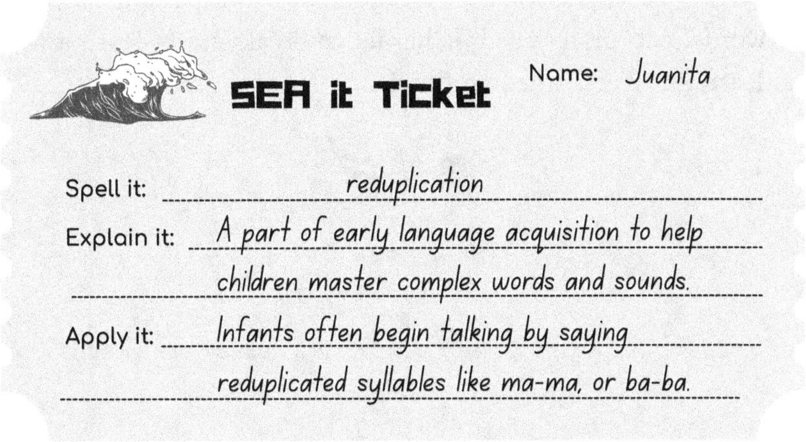

SEA it Ticket

Name: Juanita

Spell it: reduplication

Explain it: A part of early language acquisition to help children master complex words and sounds.

Apply it: Infants often begin talking by saying reduplicated syllables like ma-ma, or ba-ba.

You can download a blank copy of this *SEA It* Ticket in the appendices on page 195.

2. All the Words Around

Students are given a few short texts/sentences that include a specific technical term which has been explicitly taught. Students highlight all the other words within the passages that are being used to describe or explain the term being discussed or explained. Students list these words and then write their own sentences using these descriptive and informative words.

Alternatively, students can explore their own writing to see what words they are currently using to describe and explain the technical word and brainstorm different words they could use to revise their writing. The class could also brainstorm words that might be used and write sentences with these or use a worked example of the final product to identify the words beyond (or around) the technical concept. This can sometimes include verbs as well.

Be prepared for students to be working with potentially (and hopefully!) unfamiliar terms. Consider ways to support their experimentation with these words and be sure to correct misconceptions (around spelling, connotation or function) throughout the activity. Teachers don't want students to orthographically map new words inaccurately, as it is harder to break and re-learn a word than learn it correctly the first time!

Classroom example

All the Words Around

1. Read the following passages and **highlight** all the descriptive and informative words being used to explain the concept of visual salience.

Text #1: Visual salience refers to the distinctiveness or prominence of an object or feature in a visual scene that makes it stand out and capture attention. This distinctiveness can be influenced by factors such as colour, contrast, brightness and motion, allowing certain elements to draw our focus while other fade into the background. Understanding visual salience helps explain how we process visual information and how attention is allocated in complex scenes, which is crucial for effective perception. (Fiveable, n.d.)

Text #2: Salience is how much any section of an image draws the viewer's eyes - the most salient feature of an image is whatever/wherever the viewer's eyes are first drawn when they look at it. Salience is always deliberate and usually created through contrast, colour, framing and layout. (Art of Smart, 2025)

Text #3: Salience refers to focus. Due to its inherent visual nature, it is more difficult to implement in a literary medium. Salience is when the creator, through the use of various techniques such as colour and form, makes a particular object, person or group stand out. This is essentially achieved through contrast. By creating a uniform image and then having something specific differ from the rest, our eyes are naturally drawn to it. (Wharton, 2023)

2. Use the words you have highlighted to write one sentence that **describes** and **explains** the concept of visual salience and another sentence that uses visual salience to **analyse** a visual.

Describe: *Visually salient features capture the attention of the viewer by using colour, contrast, brightness or layout to draw a viewer's eyes to crucial elements.*

Analyse: *Through deliberate framing and contrast, the visual salience of the image establishes the difference between the central figure and the background, allowing the subject to stand out prominently, while muted tones in the surrounding elements fade into the background to reinforce the inherent importance for the viewer to connect with the subject.*

You can download a blank copy of the *All the Words Around* worksheet in the appendices on page 195.

3. 10 Most Important Words

Students brainstorm (either as a class, in groups or individually) the *10 Most Important Words* from a specific unit (or subtopic). Once complete, students can debate why they chose those words (over other words) and write sentences, using as many of the words in the list as possible, which highlight their relationship and significance.

Classroom example

A table, such as Figure 2.6, can be altered so the ranking is omitted (if that isn't important) or the final column can be used to connect the concept to an example of any application of the word that is desired.

Teachers can also provide students (some or all) with the *10 Most Important Words* (often technical terms of a unit) and ask them (individually, or in groups) to clarify and prioritise these terms.

The second and third columns of the table can easily be cut out, folded in half and used as flash cards for revision.

Figure 2.6: Example *10 Most Important Words* table

	Word	Meaning	Why it got this ranking?
1	law	a set of rules everyone must follow	they keep everyone safe
2	justice	treating people fairly and applying the law properly	is what the law aims to create
3	rights	things people are allowed to do or have	is what the law is based upon
4	crime	breaking the law	what happens when people don't follow the law
5	court	the place where legal cases and decisions are made	where the law is enacted
6	judge	the person who leads the court and makes decisions	the person who uses the law to create justice
7	legislation	the specific laws that are made and put into effect	the result and consequence of the law
8	punishment	negative actions enforced by a judge	what happens when someone breaks the law
9	democracy	a system where people get to vote for leaders and laws	how citizens can have a say in the law
10	appeal	asking a court to reconsider a decision if it seems unfair	ensures mistakes in court are fixed and justice served

You can download a blank copy of the *10 Most Important Words* table in the appendices on page 195.

4. Word Sums and Matrices

Students are asked to break a word into its 'meaningful' parts – considering any prefixes, base/root words and suffixes being used to create the word. By looking at the meaning of each part, students

Connecting vocabulary

better understand the subtleties of the overall definition and can chunk the spelling more effectively.

Word Sums can be an excellent way for students to understand not only a word's **denotation** (literal meaning) but its spelling patterns and potential **derivations** (ways to change a word's function – from a verb to a noun, for example) as well. By physically exploring the word, it is much easier for students to connect the word into their long-term memory and, therefore, active vocabulary.

Classroom examples

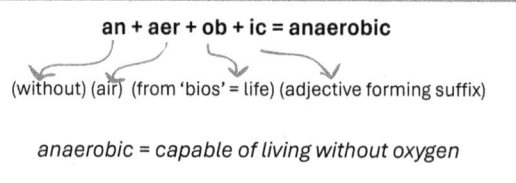

an + aer + ob + ic = anaerobic

(without) (air) (from 'bios' = life) (adjective forming suffix)

anaerobic = capable of living without oxygen

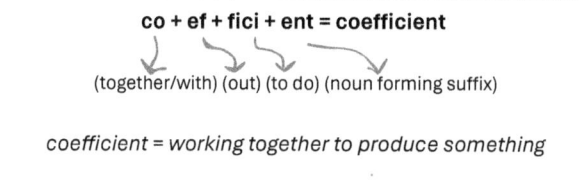

co + ef + fici + ent = coefficient

(together/with) (out) (to do) (noun forming suffix)

coefficient = working together to produce something

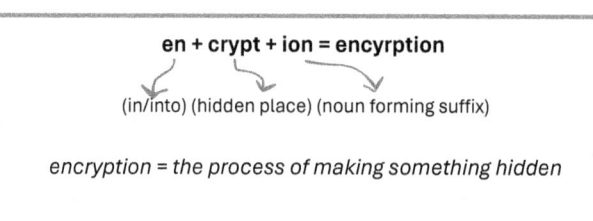

en + crypt + ion = encyrption

(in/into) (hidden place) (noun forming suffix)

encryption = the process of making something hidden

You can download copies of *Common Prefixes* and *Common Suffixes* lists in the appendices on page 195.

While breaking new terms down into a *Word Sum* is a highly valuable vocabulary strategy, building *Word Sums* from lists of affixes and base words, or through *Word Matrices*, can be excellent bell-ringers/primers, brain breaks or exit slip activities that promote vocabulary development.

These word-building (morphological) activities extend *Word Sums* as a way for students to consider relationships between words and how words can be built from different meaningful parts. *Matrices* are 'read' from left to right, where prefixes in the left column/s are added to the base word, and any number of suffixes in the right column/s are added at the end (see Figure 2.7). Not all combinations create real words and columns cannot be 'jumped' to build words.

Students can be provided with a *Matrix* or *Word Builder* to see how many words can be created – or they can be given a base/root word to then brainstorm different affixes that could be attached to create new words.

Classroom examples

Figure 2.7: Example *Word Matrix*

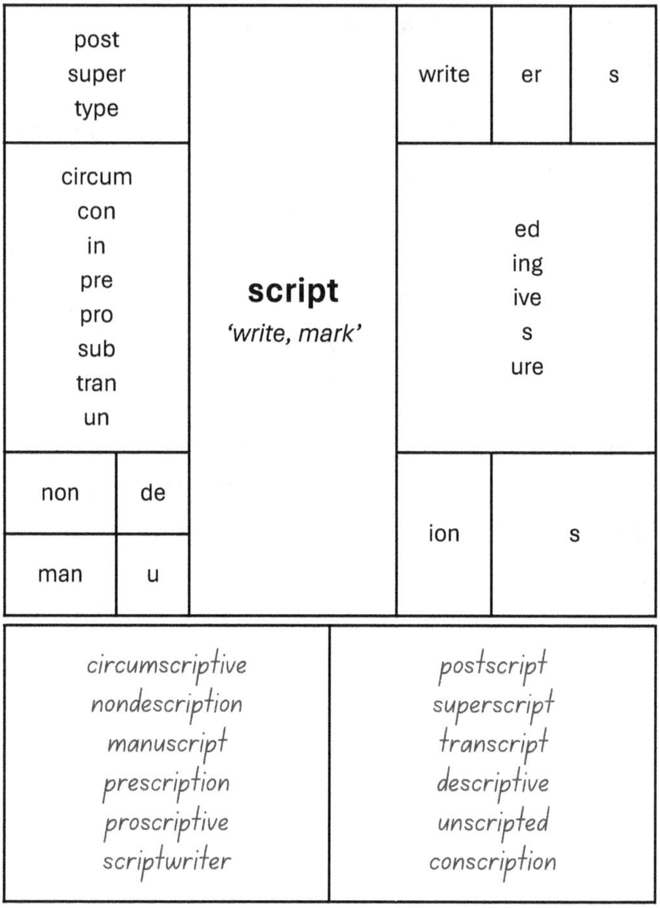

post super type			write	er	s
circum con in pre pro sub tran un		**script** *'write, mark'*		ed ing ive s ure	
non	de				
			ion		s
man	u				
circumscriptive *nondescription* *manuscript* *prescription* *proscriptive* *scriptwriter*			*postscript* *superscript* *transcript* *descriptive* *unscripted* *conscription*		

Figure 2.8: Example *Word Builder*

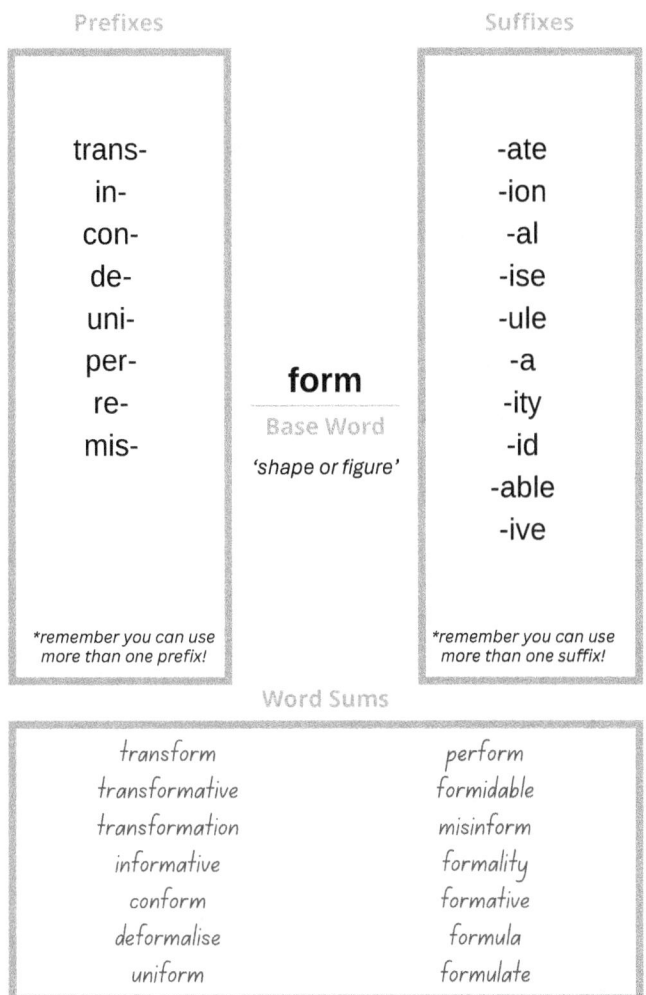

You can download a blank copy of the *Word Builder* worksheet in the appendices on page 195.

5. Graphic organiser templates

One of the most recognised word organisers is the *Frayer Model* template, which explores different elements of a word. There are, however, numerous templates, or ways to revise the templates, to prioritise the important aspects of a word and how students need to connect and engage with the words being explored.

Any graphic organiser template can be used in small-group, individual or homework situations. The bonus of graphic organisers is that they can categorise the information in ways that students can then use purposefully, and categories can be changed depending on the relevance to the word and how students will need to use it.

Classroom examples

The act of handwriting on worksheets extends the opportunity for long-term learning to occur. Wherever possible, ask students to write answers in full sentences using a capital letter and end mark (they need to automate the way they use punctuation as well, but more of that in Chapter 4).

Figure 2.9: Example *Frayer Model*

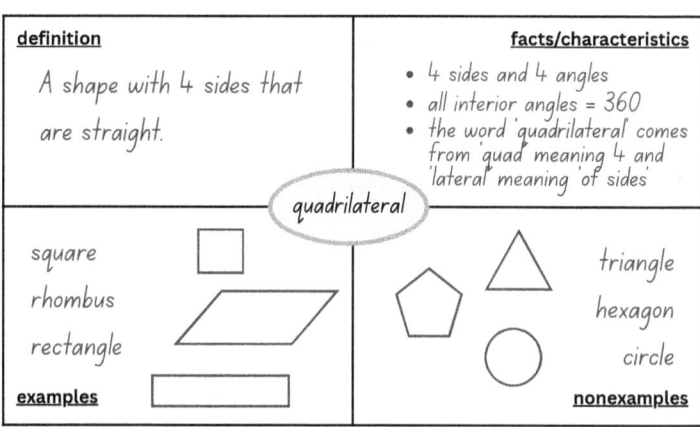

Figure 2.10: Example *Word Investigation*

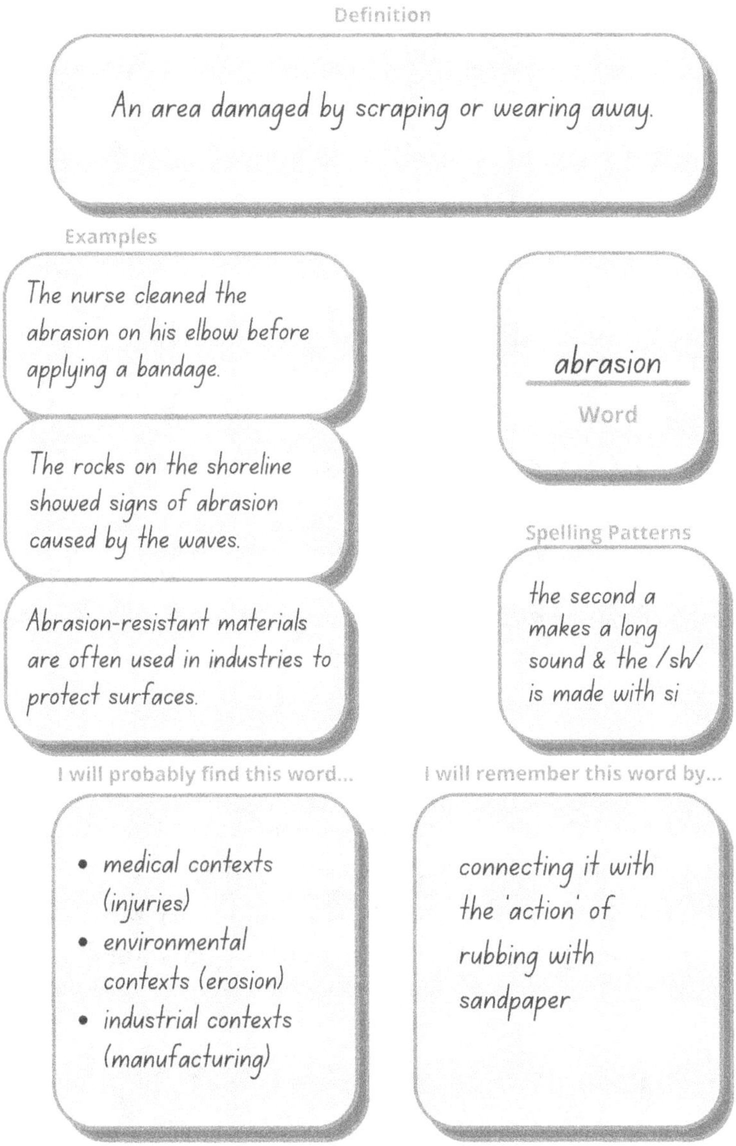

Definition

An area damaged by scraping or wearing away.

Examples

The nurse cleaned the abrasion on his elbow before applying a bandage.

The rocks on the shoreline showed signs of abrasion caused by the waves.

Abrasion-resistant materials are often used in industries to protect surfaces.

Word

abrasion

Spelling Patterns

the second a makes a long sound & the /sh/ is made with si

I will probably find this word...

- medical contexts (injuries)
- environmental contexts (erosion)
- industrial contexts (manufacturing)

I will remember this word by...

connecting it with the 'action' of rubbing with sandpaper

Figure 2.11: Example *Word Clarifying* worksheet

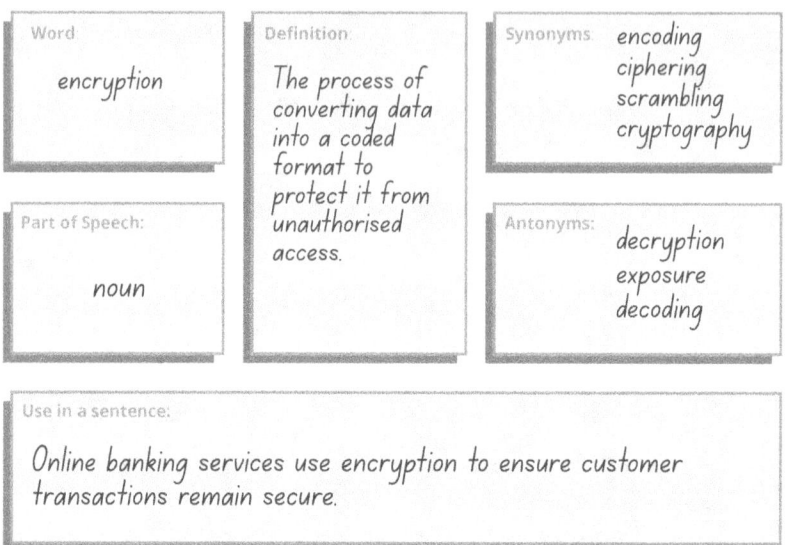

You can download blank copies of the *Word Investigation* and *Word Clarifying* worksheets in the appendices on page 195.

Many vocabulary activities can be turned into engaging or even competitive opportunities where 'challenge words' are displayed, and students can be rewarded when using a word correctly. Words are fun and powerful, but we don't use them in isolation, so ensure you give them the respect and time they deserve, and don't waste time on a single word when you can explore numerous words simultaneously!

Connect: from page to practice

Looking through a specific unit of work and a student sample of the final summative task:

1. List all the technical (tier 3) and academic (tier 2) vocabulary required or relevant for the unit. Use an exemplar student sample to identify the types of additional words required for students to best find success.

2. Work through your current curriculum documentation and consider where and how you can explicitly (or implicitly) teach these terms. Focus on the balance between the technical and academic words and how they work together.

3. Consider which vocabulary activities or resources might work best in explicitly teaching, supporting, consolidating and extending new vocabulary and embed these into the curriculum purposefully.

Remember: Adding extensive vocabulary lists to your documentation isn't often helpful in the application of these words into the classroom. Consider bolding terms that require explicit teaching and highlighting supporting vocabulary that would be worthwhile in modelling and maximising exposure to these words as well as recognising when they may need to be explicitly taught. You need to be able to see where the word will be used in your lesson, rather than create a detached list in your curriculum that you then have to try and remember to somehow connect in the moment.

Connecting vocabulary... in summary

Teaching vocabulary
Explicitly teaching vocabulary supports students' learning, their ability to read and comprehend and to write and articulate their understanding. It is the fundamental first step to unlocking the language we use to communicate.

Building vocabulary
Teachers don't necessarily need to understand the science behind the orthographic mapping that occurs when learning new words, but they do need to understand the skills students use to decode (read) and encode (spell) unfamiliar terms.

**Two vocabularies
Three tiers
Countless exposures**
Everyone has both a **passive** and an **active** vocabulary: the difference between words that are understood when reading or listening versus words that are used when speaking or writing.

Vocabulary can be classified into **3 tiers**: everyday (tier 1), academic (tier 2, including command terms) and technical (tier 3).

A person needs numerous exposures to map a word into their passive vocabulary and significantly more before it can become a part of their active vocabulary.

More than a word

Remember, vocabulary teaching shouldn't only focus on technical (tier 3) words or a single word in isolation. Students need to consider how words work together and experiment with how they can be applied in a variety of contexts.

Every class, every day

Remember to consider ways every class can provide a vocabulary-rich environment for students to learn, experiment with, consolidate and apply the plethora of words available to them.

Beyond the definition

It is not enough to simply provide a definition of a word for students to then absorb into their vocabulary. Students need to be able to:
- **pronounce** the word (so they can use it in their spoken vocabulary)
- **spell** the word (so they can use it in their written vocabulary)
- understand the **connotations** of the word (so they can use it in appropriate ways and contexts)
- **change** the word (so they can use it in a variety of ways)

Connecting Whole-School Literacy in the Secondary Context

Chapter 3
Connecting reading

Key chapter concept: *As a predominantly internal skill, it can be difficult to determine where misunderstandings in reading originate. Teachers need to identify the potential complexity of the reading demands they place on their students and draw from a variety of strategies at a word, sentence or text level to not only check for student understanding, but to help students monitor for meaning, synthesise across a text and extend their reading into more sophisticated thinking.*

The skills to read

There are innumerable studies into how an individual learns to read, yet the 'Reading Wars' continue to rage around the most effective ways to teach reading in Australia and across the world. Seeped in a complex history, much of the controversy centres on the foundational and initial processes to teach reading. These debates around Whole Language versus Systematic Phonics Instruction seem somewhat irrelevant in the secondary context. The assumption remains that students 'should be able to read' by the time they reach Year 7, and therefore the focus on reading development at high school sits in building students' comprehension and their ability to process, synthesise and analyse a variety of increasingly sophisticated texts.

The reality, however, is that many students reach Year 7 (and beyond) without the foundational reading skills required to comprehend year-level texts. Initially, this is most often interpreted as a comprehension issue, but this simplistic perspective does not allow for the huge variance in where reading misunderstanding can originate.

Gough and Tunmer's (1986) original formula, *The Simple View of Reading* (Figure 3.0), was expanded in 1992 by Dr Hollis Scarborough to visually demonstrate the various subskills within word recognition and language comprehension. Through *The Reading Rope* (Figure 3.2), she emphasised the importance of the different 'strands' becoming increasingly automatic and strategic as they 'weaved' together into a strong 'rope' of skilled reading. This graphic has been revised in semantic ways by other individuals, but all interpretations highlight the impact specific skills have in disrupting or supporting overall comprehension.

Figure 3.0: *The Simple View of Reading* formula

$$\text{word recognition} \times \text{language comprehension} = \text{skilled reading}$$

Figure 3.1: *The Simple View of Writing* formula

$$\text{transcription} \times \text{language processessing} = \text{skilled writing}$$

Figure 3.2: *The Reading Rope* graphic

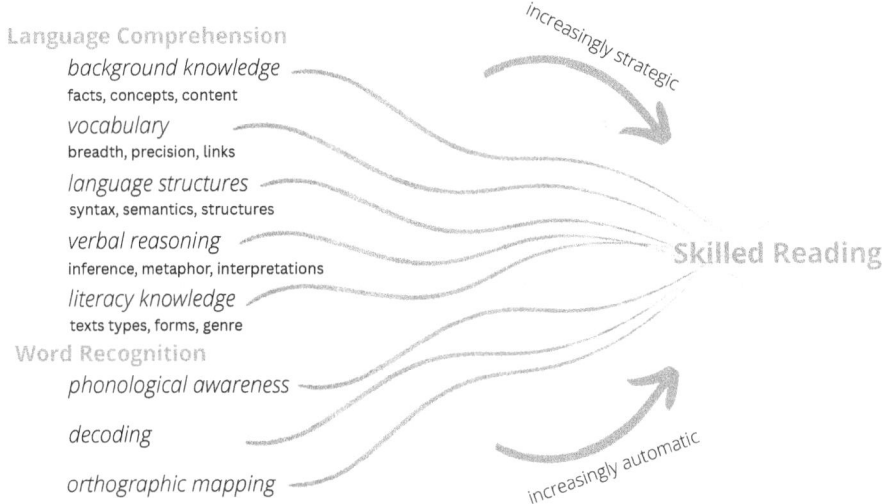

Considering the individual skills required for effective reading, it is important for teachers to recognise how comprehension of a reading task may be broken due to several factors, such as:

- The student might not have the *background knowledge* or *vocabulary* to make sense of the text.
- They might become confused by the *structure* and way the information is presented, the *construction* of sentences or the *purpose* of the text.
- They could come unstuck in their ability to *decode* unfamiliar words or interpret the *connotations* or *punctuation* being used to create tone, inference and meaning.

While any teacher (other than an English teacher) might not need to know what is specifically holding a student back from comprehending a text, understanding the variety of reasons why a student might be confused by a reading demand allows teachers to make more informed decisions around the different strategies and scaffolds they can put into place to help any number of students in their class.

Skilled reading is not an isolated skill but the result of numerous skills working in collaboration.

> **QUESTIONS TO CONNECT**
> - What does 'skilled reading' look like in the context of your subject/s and class/es?
> - What specific reading skills do you notice students struggling with while reading in your classes?
> - How confident are you in identifying and supporting these individual skills?

Reading demands

A Deakin University study (Rutherford et al., 2024) found almost three in ten students in Years 7–12 said they did not read in their spare time and that "curriculum pressures also meant students were given less time to read in class as they moved into senior school levels". While reading has been linked to numerous studies proving its benefit beyond the classroom, too often the pressure and concept of providing time to 'read for pleasure' takes precedence in reading intervention programs. Teachers who do not engage with narrative texts, therefore, don't see the relevance or impact upon the reading demands in their classes.

Initially, there is a reason why 'reading for pleasure' is prioritised. The link between reading widely and school performance is well-established, but there is significant research that exposes the correlation between reading engagement and levels of attainment most accurately applies to those students who read fiction (Jerrim & Moss, 2019).

Maryanne Wolf (2008) describes this phenomenon as *The Fiction Effect*, where she highlights how the "deeper reading" required when reading fiction is demanding enough that, over time, it reshapes the brain's neural pathways to increase its capacity to analyse, reason and understand.

McCallum (2025) considers the impact of *The Fiction Effect* in the classroom and recommends schools focus on:

- developing *interest and engagement* in reading fiction
- creating classroom approaches to develop *deep reading cognitive processes*
- building *personal connections and responses* to reading
- not getting distracted from the *purpose* (for example, disrupting reading to 'learn new words' – vocabulary development pertains much more to non-fiction reading).

Yet, schools (and life) require more than fiction reading. Lawrence (2021) exposes how reading demands in different disciplines "tend to place differential demands on students". He proposes teachers "need to support discipline-specific reading skills" in their subjects and then help students to "understand which skills to emphasise strategically". To highlight this importance, he compared the different ways Scarborough's *Reading Rope* could be interpreted depending on the subject-specific reading demand. This concept has been adapted in Table 3.0 to highlight how the same skills of *The Reading Rope* can look entirely different (depending on the subject) and why students are likely to find transferring these vital skills between units of work difficult enough, let alone transferring these skills between different classes.

So, while reading fiction throughout the secondary context should be emphasised, the subject-specific reading demands need to be identified, acknowledged and explicitly prioritised across the school.

Table 3.0: Subject-specific reading skills, categorised into *Reading Rope* subskills

Reading Rope subskill	Food Technology	History	Literature
Background knowledge	cooking methods, nutrition, food safety principles	historical events, cultural contexts, societal shifts	the canon, genre, author influence, historical context
Vocabulary	culinary terms, procedural and informative terms	historical terms, events, people, places, dates	literary terms, archaic or poetic language
Language structures	sequencing and procedural descriptions	chronological sequencing, analysis and interpretations of sources	varied sentence structures and dialogue conventions
Verbal reasoning	interpreting and adjusting recipes, predicting ingredient interactions	evaluating perspectives, analysing sources, identifying bias, drawing connections	inferring themes, analysing characters, building interpretations
Literacy knowledge	menus, recipes, packaging labels, nutritional charts	historical documents, primary and secondary sources, timelines, maps	intertextuality, varied text structures and conventions (novels, plays, poetry)

Reading Rope subskill	Maths	Physical Education	Science
Background knowledge	mathematical principles and exposure to a variety of methods and concepts	sports, human anatomy, fitness principles	scientific concepts, real-word applications, experimental processes
Vocabulary	technical and non-technical mathematical terms	body/movement-based terms, procedural and informative	scientific terms, procedural language
Language structures	symbolic expressions, precise definitions, logical sequencing	instructional and procedural language, definitions, precise expression	succinct and precise expression, passive voice
Verbal reasoning	identifying patterns, understanding word problems, applying logic	understanding tactical plays, interpreting programs, connecting information to real-life situations	drawing conclusions, evaluating hypotheses, applying reasoning
Literacy knowledge	reading equations, graphs, figures, maths-specific formats	fitness guides, rule sheets, performance data	varied presentations of data (tables, graphs, figures), lab reports

Sometimes, however, teachers can begin to see reading in their class as only the extended or assessable texts students engage with for extended periods. The reality of the amount of reading students complete over the course of any school day, though, can be astounding. Table 3.1 provides a list of potential reading a student might be required to engage in across different subjects, contexts and situations in a school day.

Table 3.1: Potential reading forms in a secondary context

newspaper and online articles	worked examples	textbooks	reference books
websites	questions	board notes	checklists
novels and short stories	scripts	graphic novels or comics	poetry
autobiographies or biographies	online classroom pages	criteria, rubrics and assessment	handouts and worksheets
instructions, recipes	brochures, pamphlets, posters	quizzes	emails, newsletters, noticeboards

While this list is far from exhaustive, or specific, it is interesting to note how important reading skills are to navigate through life – and not just in an academic sense. If schools can begin to recognise the vital role that reading has across any given day, then teachers are much more likely to be increasingly conscious about ways to support students in building their reading capacities.

This all being said, in a world of social media and text messages, it is important that students are supported to build the stamina and resilience to read extended texts and for extended periods of time. If students are only ever exposed to excerpts, worksheets, posters and emails, there is little surprise when they struggle to stay engaged and have the reading stamina to process longer or more complex reading material.

Added to this are the negative effects of reading in digital formats. While the increasing access and reliance on technology has seen young people reading more than ever before, this reading averages less than a minute per text. They are browsing, scanning and skimming; reading widely but not deeply. Salmerón et al. (2023) reveal that reading in a digital form negatively correlates with reading comprehension, and digital reading does not develop print reading skills – but the opposite is in fact true.

Therefore, the more complex the reading demand, the more important it is to be read in the physical, rather than digital, form.

So, teachers need to do more than simply identify the reading demands being placed upon their students. To understand how best to support students in any given reading, the *complexity* of that reading demand needs to be considered. The complexity of a text will depend on several potential factors that can be categorised as either fixed or variable.

Fixed factors are those the writer has decided (or the task has determined) in creating the piece. These include:	**Variable factors** are those the reader brings with them that impact the way they engage and ultimately understand the text. These include:
• word length • format, font size and type • text type and form • register and lexical density • vocabulary • purpose (the reason the text was written).	• background knowledge (of the content text type, form and vocabulary) • motivation and engagement (their desire to read and understand the text) • reading fluency and working memory capacity.

When determining the potential support for reading a text, the teacher needs to consider the impact of both fixed and variable complexity factors for different students. Depending on the elements with the highest impact, the most effective strategy for support is likely to be different for each text.

For example:

- An extended, highly academic text is likely to need vocabulary explained, and processing organisers to help annotate and interpret the text.
- In contrast, a checklist will more likely require supporting students to see the benefit and purpose of the reading to initiate actions. Such a reading will require consideration of the background experience of those students who might not have used a checklist before in this context, or students who will need reminding to continue to go back and re-engage with the checklist periodically.

> **QUESTIONS TO CONNECT**
>
> - What reading demands do you place on your students beyond the assessable tasks, and how complex are these demands?
> - Which reading demands do you explicitly scaffold and support, and which do you assume students should be able to access independently?
> - What type of reading contexts do your students generally find the most difficult?

Assessing comprehension

One of the great complexities in the education system is the fact that student understanding is most often assessed through writing. Using this method, however, makes it almost impossible for a teacher to ascertain if a misunderstanding has been caused by a reading misconception or limitations in the writing skills required to articulate the understanding accurately.

The first thing to consider, then, is how teachers can 'assess' reading, comprehension and student understanding of content. The following five strategies highlight different ways teachers can attempt to discover if a student has understood a text or not, so they can then determine how to support the student more effectively.

---

1. Check for Understanding Activities

The concept of *Check for Understanding Activities* is far from new but has had a growing resurgence of importance recently as a way to support explicit teaching and feedback practices. There are innumerable individual strategies a teacher can select from, but the principles of any *Check for Understanding Activities* should:

- take minimal planning, preparation or class time
- involve *every* student actively providing their response
- allow the teacher to ascertain levels of understanding and highlight misconceptions or confusions that require subsequent reclarification or teaching.

Some engaging and effective *Check for Understanding Activities* include:

a. **Four words and a statement** – students identify four words that reflect the key concepts of a reading and then use those four words in a summary sentence/statement.

b. **Mini-whiteboards (or simply paper)** – each student writes their response to a question and lifts their board (in an action known as *Chin It*) to show the teacher at the same time.

c. **Multiple-choice fingers** – students place their fist on their chest and then raise the appropriate number of fingers that corresponds to a multiple-choice question.

d. **One fact, one question** – students write one thing they have learned and one question they have after reading.

e. **Yes/no cards** – students have (or create) a paper with YES on one side and NO on the other and raise the appropriate answer when asked a closed question. This can also be done as open or closed hands on chest.

2. Spoken Responses

Speaking and listening, as core literacy skills identified in Chapter 1, are significantly easier than reading (or writing) as they are innate skills rather than requiring explicit learning. As such, being able to discuss a reading can allow students to process and consolidate their understanding, while at the same time clarifying or identifying misconceptions.

Beyond the five speaking and listening strategies outlined in Chapter 1 that can be adapted to discuss and explore a reading, other spoken responses that can be used to help students process a reading – or for teachers to assess their understanding – include:

- **Any partnered, small-group or whole-class discussion:** including *Partner Talk, Sage and Scribe, Listening Triangles, Turn and Talk* or *Think-Pair-Share* activities. See *Activating Prior Knowledge* activities for further explanation on these and other potential activities in the appendices on page 195.
- **Reciprocal Reading:** in small groups, students read an excerpt/text together and each take responsibility in one specific focus area. This might include elements such as highlighting/clarifying key vocabulary, summarising key ideas, visualising the information through creating a graphic representation, connecting the information to the wider unit being discussed, identifying evidence, etc. Students are given time to explore, discuss, question and respond to the text together.
- **Hot Seat Interviews:** students take on the persona of a person, concept or perspective based on a reading and, from that perspective, answer questions asked by the class.
- **Panel Discussions:** a group of students come to the front and each take a different perspective or persona from a specific reading they have completed. They are then interviewed by the rest of the class on a topic. In this way, they become 'experts' on the content of the text they have read.
- **On-the-Fence Debates:** the class is split into two and each group is given a different reading on the same topic. Then the groups are positioned on opposite sides of the room and asked to take turns providing different opinions and evidence to support their team's point of view on a topic, based on the reading they completed.
- **Cumulative Brainstorms:** in groups or individually, students complete different readings on the same topic. They then take turns in building upon another student's idea with either

evidence, another idea or an alternative perspective, supported by their text. This can also be completed initially as a *Sticky Note Slam* (see the appendices on page 195) and then groups can categorise and synthesise the ideas into one cohesive response. See *Activating Prior Knowledge* activities in the appendices as well, for further details on this or other potential activities.

3. Reading Organisers

There are any number of graphic organisers that can be used to process, clarify and synthesise reading material. The trick is to match the graphic organiser with what the students need to know or do after the reading. Teachers need to be confident to adjust organisers to not only suit the reading, but support what the student needs to 'do' with the information from the reading afterwards.

Some of the most common and effective *Reading Organisers* include:

- *Concept, Cluster* or *Spider Maps*
- *Venn Diagrams* or *T-Chart Tables*
- *Hierarchy* or *Network Trees*
- *Lotus Diagrams*
- *Timelines, Cycles* or *Sequence Charts*
- *Learning Logs, KWLH Graphs* or *Matrices*.

You can download blank copies of a *Selection of Reading Organisers* in the appendices on page 195.

4. Summaries

Being able to summarise a text is one of the most important, yet difficult tasks teachers can ask students to complete after reading. It can mistakenly be assumed that summarising is a simple way to process a text and allow students to show their understanding of what they have read. But the skills of summarising are significant and require explicit instruction. This does not mean teachers shouldn't use *Summaries* to assess student understanding, but rather they need to recognise the writing demands being placed upon students when asking them to complete such tasks.

When setting summarising tasks, it is important to:

- Be explicit with the length and form of the summary (dot points, single sentence, short paragraph, etc.).
- Consider the audience and purpose of the summary (simply showing their understanding, explaining the concept to another person, creating study notes, etc.).
- Scaffold the writing by potentially providing key words to be included; how many points/sentences should be included; guidelines around using technical language; or different types of sentence frames that can be used.
- Extend the writing by challenging students to say the same thing but in fewer words; increase the register by including more formal (tier 2) vocabulary; embed quotes throughout; or consider more sophisticated **conjunctions** (words that join clauses*, phrases* or words within a sentence, for example, 'and', 'but', 'because') and **connectives** (words or phrases that link ideas across or within sentences, for example, 'however', 'as a result').

---

* A **clause** is a group of words that expresses a complete idea with a subject and a verb. A **phrase** is a group of words that work together as a unit without a subject-verb pair.

Some summarising activities include:

- **Big Idea, Supporting Detail:** students identify the main idea of a text and then list three to five points that are either supporting or providing detail about the main idea. They can then be given sentence starters (for example, 'The main idea is… This is supported by…') to use their identified elements to construct a summary of the text.
- **60-Second Summary:** students write some dot points about the text and then have a minute to explain the text to a partner, group or the class. The other students can then be challenged to write a summary from the student's description before reading the text themselves and seeing if their summary was accurate. Students can also record the summary and then edit the transcript of the recording into a formal written statement.
- **Jigsaw Summary:** in groups, individual students are allocated a specific section of a text to summarise. After each student shares back, the group collaboratively reconstructs a summary of the text in its entirety.
- **Summary vs Opinion:** students are asked to write a factual summary of a text. They are then asked to write a personal opinion on or an evaluation of the same text. Placing the two responses side by side, students can then identify similarities and differences in vocabulary and language features.
- **Summary Pyramid:** challenge students to summarise a text with:
    - one word (topic)
    - two words (main idea)
    - three words (key detail)
    - four words (another detail)
    - five words (the text's purpose or effect).

Classroom examples

Summary Pyramid

Text: *The Role of Dynamics in Musical Expression*

- dynamics
- volume changes
- crescendo, decrescendo, contrast
- shapes atmosphere and interpretation
- conveys meaning, building desired emotion

Text: *The Lottery* by Shirley Jackson	
theme	tradition
main idea	blind obedience
key event	annual village ritual
key detail	violence masked as normality
author's intention	critiquing impact of unquestioned norms

5. Note Making and Annotations

Making notes while reading (or after the initial reading) allows students time to process what has been read and place it into their own words (or visuals) to better recall the information later. The difference between *Note Taking* and where students simply quote directly from a text, means *Note Making* requires explicit teaching and scaffolding before students are confident and capable of completing the process independently. As a skill, though, it is a powerful academic tool to gift students that is worth the investment.

Initially, it will involve supporting students to **annotate** (mark up) a text. *Annotations* can include any underline, highlight, symbol or word written on a text that can be used to identify, synthesise and make sense of a text. This might include:

- numbering the paragraphs or ideas
- drawing lines or arrows between connected ideas or elements
- labelling connections, key concepts or examples
- highlighting key or unfamiliar words
- writing questions or question-marking confusing parts
- colour coding information or structural features to categorise elements.

Annotations can allow teachers to see how a student connects to a reading, what they identify as important and how they draw connections across a text. It is also the first step for students to 'see' the way a text is constructed.

Building from *Annotations*, *Note Making* can then involve different ways students can process and synthesise the elements they have identified in their *Annotations*, including:

- creating visual representations of the material
- categorising and synthesising the information into like or contrasting groups

- finding synonyms or alternative ways to paraphrase and express concepts
- sequencing the time, location or concepts together
- asking clarifying, extension and reflection questions.

When asking students to undertake *Note Making*, it is important to provide different ways for students to express their understanding. While a teacher can model and allow students to experiment with visual representations or sequencing strategies, including suggested graphic organisers, the goal is for students to find a strategy that best supports the way their brain most easily processes written information and something they can replicate independently.

Ultimately, teachers need to be prepared to allow students to access reading in different ways and consider different opportunities to assess their comprehension and application of such reading. Rather than using reading assessment to find the 'right' answer, teachers should create opportunities to actively look for any misconceptions that can be explained and clarified effectively.

QUESTIONS TO CONNECT

- How are you currently assessing students' understanding of the reading they are completing in your class?
- How often are you assessing every student's understanding versus the cohort collectively?
- Do you always check for reading understanding in the same way? What other ways could you check more effectively or regularly?

Common reading difficulties and relevant support strategies

As seen in *The Reading Rope* (see page 75), there are many competing skills that may contribute to a student's confusion when reading. The following are some of the most common reading gaps, confusions and areas for improvement that teachers are likely to encounter when asking students to read in their classes.

For each reading issue, some specific supporting strategies and considerations to experiment with have been included as well as a more detailed activity that can be layered against certain reading demands when struggles with these skills are blocking students from accessing the information required.

---

1. Decoding, phonemic awareness and fluency gaps

Some students will struggle to pronounce (and often spell) new or unfamiliar words; or they might not read with enough pace or expression to help make meaning from the words they are reading. As such, these students will need support to firstly decode and then connect this vocabulary into the context of the reading. Other students will need modelling and opportunities to practise reading aloud and for meaning. This doesn't necessarily mean getting struggling readers to read aloud to the class but rather allowing opportunities to read alongside or practise reading before discussing or responding.

Supporting strategies:

- As discussed in Chapter 2, it is vital when introducing new vocabulary that teachers don't just provide glossaries or focus on the definition of unfamiliar words. Prioritise that every student can pronounce unfamiliar words (and spell them).
- Modelling correct pronunciation and connecting the sounds of the word with its definition will not only support a student to

understand and use new vocabulary but also models ways for students to decode future unfamiliar words independently.

- Modelling appropriate expression and pace when reading aloud, such as using punctuation and phrasing purposefully, brings the written word to 'life' and demonstrates how a person 'hears' a text when they read. Drawing attention to the punctuation or phrases used helps demystify the process for many students.

Supporting activity: **Repeated, Partnered or Performance Reading**

Providing students different ways to access reading can mean individuals begin recognising what is most helpful for them to understand a text. Reading a text multiple times in different ways can also illuminate the benefit of re-reading for meaning. For example, students could:

- Read the text silently and then aloud with a partner.
- Have the text read aloud in one lesson and then be asked to read it silently to themselves in another lesson for a specific purpose.
- Record themselves reading and listen back to their recording to take notes.
- Read the text aloud as a 'performance' (this can be particularly fun if it is a dry informational or procedural text), where they overemphasise expression, punctuation and audience response.

Establishing *Repeated Reading* routines will help alleviate the perceived 'time waste' of reading a text multiple times. The concept assists students who are working on building their reading fluency and expression, but it is also a great strategy to read a text as it was intended first, and then re-read (potentially quicker, or a skim and scan) to identify key elements and consolidate understanding depending on what a reader is going to do with the information provided.

2. Vocabulary gaps and confusions

As elaborated on in Chapter 2 (see page 48), students become confused when reading texts due to the tier 2 (academic) vocabulary rather than solely the technical words included. They might get the gist of a text through the tier 3 words that have been explicitly taught and their understanding of tier 1 words, but will often miss the connotations, descriptions, explanations or relationships because of their limited tier 2 vocabulary.

Supporting strategies:

- When introducing technical terms, teachers need to ensure they also consider the types of descriptive words used alongside the term (the activity *All the Words Around* on page 59 does this well).
- Similarly, when clarifying vocabulary in a reading, teachers shouldn't just focus on nouns and verbs (the main elements of a sentence); they should also consider the descriptive or relational words that some students might not have encountered before or skimmed over and missed their importance.
- Establishing a culture where students are encouraged to ask and clarify unfamiliar terms they encounter while reading is crucial. It can be shocking how many words students 'read' across the day without knowing their meaning.
- Encouraging students to place a question mark next to or on top of unfamiliar terms can help them (and the teacher) to see the confusions. These words could alternatively be underlined, highlighted or written as a list alongside the reading and explored as part of the post-reading activities.

Supporting activity: **Substitute and Simplify**

This is most useful for students who are struggling with the vocabulary of a reading task, but it can be a whole-class activity for particularly complex or important texts. Students are asked to highlight any word they are either unfamiliar with or seems to be used in an unfamiliar way. They then look up the meaning and simple synonyms for the word and write the most appropriate synonym above the word in the text.

Once they have substituted all the words they need to, they can then re-read the sentence/text, only this time, reading the synonyms rather than original words to see if the piece now makes more sense. This is an opportunity to discuss the significance of word choice (a synonym can still drastically change the meaning of a sentence!) and promote the difference between formal and informal language features.

Classroom example

Task: Read the following excerpt about scientific geological dating and highlight any unfamiliar or confusing terms.

"Artefacts and other materials can be dated by observing which layer of sediments they are found in. This applies the geological principle that under normal circumstances younger layers of sediment will be deposited on top of older layers."

2. Simplify the information by substituting the most appropriate (and clear) synonym for any of the words you have highlighted and read the excerpt again.

"~~Artefacts and other materials~~ *(Things made by humans in the past)* can be ~~dated~~ *(worked out how old they are)* by observing which layer of ~~sediments~~ *(earth)* they are found in. This ~~applies~~ *(uses)* the geological ~~principle~~ *(idea)* that under normal ~~circumstances~~ *(situations)* younger layers of ~~sediment~~ *(earth)* will be ~~deposited~~ *(put)* on top of older layers."

3. Pronoun and other cohesive device confusions

While students will generally understand the meaning of **pronouns** and **conjunctions***, these tier 1 words often cause confusion when students misinterpret what words they are connecting or referring to. As these cohesive devices are critical to a text's overall coherence and show the relationships between elements across the text, they are a vital part of reading comprehension.

Supporting strategies:

- Take note when pronouns (or synonyms) are being used in place of key terms and concepts, and draw attention to these across the reading. Students can highlight all the references to a concept across a passage and then compare the different ways it is presented.
- Similarly with conjunctions, highlight how these words are showing a relationship between different elements in the text. Students can draw arrows between the different pieces and the conjunction, or they can move the conjunction, so the relationship is clearer. (Sometimes students will find it more difficult to see the relationship if the conjunction is at the start of the sentence and they have to connect back-to-back ideas.)

Supporting activity: **Connective Match**

This is most useful for when students are struggling at the sentence level or connecting information across a piece of reading. It can be particularly useful when they are trying to decipher more detailed questions and task instructions.

---

* **Pronouns** are words that reference a previous noun, for example, 'it', 'that', 'those', etc.
Conjunctions are words that connect ideas, for example, 'and', 'while', 'before', etc.

Students highlight the subject of the sentence (or any key terms within the reading) and literally draw an arrow from any pronoun, substitution (synonym or appositive) or repetition back to the original term. They can also highlight any key words that are showing time, relationship or connection and draw arrows from these words back to the different sections they are referring to.

While the final product can often look rather 'messy', the process of literally drawing connections across a text is a useful way for a teacher to visualise what is happening in a student's mind while they are reading. Some students can be encouraged to continue this practice when interpreting questions or texts independently, or in timed/high-stakes situations.

Classroom example

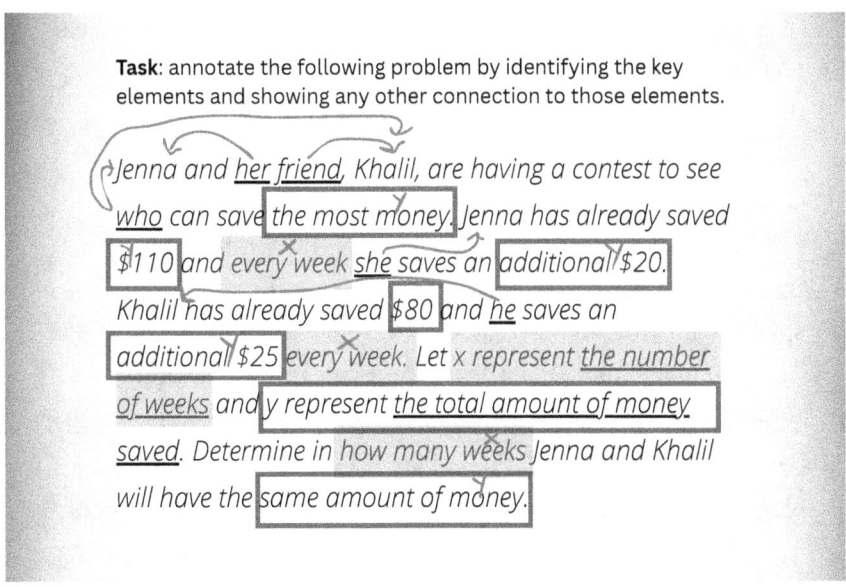

4. Comprehension – identifying and understanding literal elements

Sometimes, students simply get lost, particularly in an extended piece of reading, and struggle to identify the key elements being presented. This most often occurs when a student isn't reading deeply or purposefully, or they have low working memory and are struggling to hold all the elements together to make the meaning clear. They also might be looking for what they 'think' are the important parts, rather than reading for meaning.

Supporting strategies:

- Often, the simplest strategy is to give students the time and opportunity to slow down their reading. By emphasising that reading often needs time to process, and by rewarding the act of re-reading, students can realise that it is common to have to change the pace and the intensity of their reading depending on the text.
- While the purpose might seem obvious for teachers, some students benefit from having the reason or outcome of the reading made explicit. Do students need to understand and memorise every word, or are they looking for something specific, finding connections or evidence to support an idea? The narrower the focus, the easier it can be to interpret.
- Literal comprehension can often be supported through guided *Annotations* or *Note Making* as ways to emphasise the critical elements and help students process and synthesise for meaning.
- *Treasure Hunts* or checklists of elements to connect and consider can help some students to focus on the essential elements in more complex or extended texts.
- More general comprehension strategies include ways to support students to:
    - ask questions of the text

- change the pace of the reading (either speed up to skim and scan or slow down to identify key pieces)
- connect the punctuation to the way it helps break the text up or gives clues to the expression, meaning or emphasis
- identify the key elements of the text and connect them to the whole.

Supporting activity: **Comprehension strategies**

An internet search for 'comprehension strategies' will result in an overwhelming number of programs and 'top' strategies from around the world. It is important to be cognisant that not all reading strategies are research-supported or endorsed.

> **WHAT NOT TO DO**
>
> New Zealand teacher Marie Clay developed the *Reading Recovery* program after observing what strategies 100 'good readers' used while reading. This perspective lay the foundation for the *Whole Language* movement through the 1980s (and into today), but has been proven to be highly ineffective and even detrimental when considering the science behind how a person learns to read.
>
> Explicitly teaching comprehension strategies also gained significant traction when Dianne Snowball – who co-founded the Australian United States Services in Education (AUSSIE) reading program – took AUSSIE to New York; suddenly, students were spending their time learning how to predict, visualise, think aloud, make connections, question, infer and summarise. While these are all very worthwhile skills for students to draw from when reading, it has been proven that

explicitly teaching comprehension strategies has little to no effect on student reading outcomes (Shanahan, 2018).

While this might sound counterintuitive, the principle is to focus on *using* the strategies in different contexts and ways rather than trying to *teach* the strategies in isolation.

Therefore, schools are better to spend their time:

- Building confident readers who can *monitor their understanding* as they are reading
- Ensuring students have a variety of strategies to draw from when reading for different purposes
- Identifying which strategy might be most effective depending on the type of text and what students need to do with the information after reading.

One important thing for a student to recognise is whether they are becoming confused with a piece of reading at the *word*, *sentence* or *text level*. Once they have determined where they are struggling, they can then select the appropriate strategy to potentially help them through the reading.

By experimenting using strategies with different texts and purposes, students can independently help themselves through more complex reading tasks.

You can download a copy of the *Comprehension Strategies Handout* in the appendices on page 195.

5. Inference: reading beyond the text and making interpretations

Inferring information from a text is a significantly more complex skill than simply comprehending as it requires students to make connections and interpretations beyond the words they are reading. It requires strong vocabulary understanding (not just definitions but connotations as well) and a confidence to have an opinion that doesn't necessarily seem explicitly stated by specific words on the page.

Supporting strategies:

- Initially, inference should start at a word level – considering connotations and connectives that are highlighting relationships and perspectives. This word-level analysis can then connect from summary into interpretation.
- Students need to be comfortable to talk about their interpretations and opinions, and have clear modelling and opportunities to draw connections from the text into the other aspects of the course being studied.
- Hearing alternative perspectives is vital for students to recognise the need to bring their own ideas rather than just looking for the 'right' answer. This allows students the time to listen to and read each other's responses and celebrate the variety of appropriate answers.
- Concept maps and visual organisers can help students draw elements together and consider relationships or layer consequences or opinions over the top. (See *Graphic Organiser Templates* on page 68 and *Note Making* on page 90.)

Supporting activity: **Ask Questions to Find Answers**

Students are asked to express their confusions by writing both general and specific questions about the text they are reading. This is most useful when students are struggling to work out *why* they are finding a text difficult to understand or interpret.

Initially, the teacher explicitly models questions for the students to answer about the text and explains how that question helps to understand a text.

Some questions that can be asked of different texts include:

- Does the author have an obvious opinion about the subject? How does noticing this help us to build our own understanding of the ideas in the text?
- What evidence have they used to support their point of view? How does noticing the evidence help us to understand how the idea has been constructed?
- How does the text make you feel? How does noticing how you are feeling help us to understand the atmosphere/tone/intention of the text?
- Why did the author choose to include what they did? How does noticing the parts included help us to understand the priorities and essential elements of the text?
- What did the author choose not to include and why? How does noticing what isn't in the text help us to understand the priorities and essential elements of the text?
- Why did the author write this text? How does noticing the purpose of a text help us to understand what we are supposed to be thinking and doing after reading it?

The goal is for students to be able to question the text themselves. This can involve exploring the rationale, purpose, author bias, alternate perspectives and other higher-order thinking elements, but it can also involve literal or inferential questions around elements of the text that the student is finding confusing.

Giving students time to ask questions of a text and supporting the different types of questions that can be asked can not only help a student understand a text more deeply but also build curiosity and expression to discover the truth within the text more broadly.

It must be remembered, however, that asking questions can be difficult for some students, so teachers need to be prepared to scaffold different ways of asking them, such as using a *Question Creation Table*, such as Table 3.2.

These question-creation activities can then be:

- answered, mixed and shared across the class
- used as study tools (such as flashcards by writing the answer on the back)
- classified into like topics with the answers expanded into paragraphs
- used as retrieval practice activities, entry or exit slip cards, a class pop quiz or any number of question-response tasks.

> **QUESTIONS TO CONNECT**
>
> - What skills do you most often see your students struggling with when reading different texts in your class?
> - What strategies can you use to support them more purposefully?
> - Which strategies would differentiate best to support and extend all learners, rather than simply supporting your most struggling readers?

Classroom example

Use the *Question Creation Table* (overleaf) to write as many questions as you can about the article your group read about food safety regulations.

Table 3.2: Example Question Creation Table

	is	did	can	would	will	might
who	Who is responsible for enforcing food safety regulations in Australia?	Who did the new regulations impact the most?	Who can benefit from food safety regulations?	Who would be impacted if these regulations were not followed?	Who will conduct inspections to ensure compliance?	Who might face consequences for violating food safety rules?
what	What is the purpose of food safety regulations?	What did the new regulations seek to prevent?	What can businesses do to ensure food safety compliance?	What would happen if food safety rules were ignored?	What will be required from food suppliers under these regulations?	What might be some challenges in maintaining food safety standards?
where	Where is food safety legislation most strictly enforced in Australia?	Where did examples of foodborne illnesses occur that led to stricter regulations?	Where can food safety training courses be accessed in Australia?	Where would food safety violations be most likely to occur?	Where will inspections happen ensuring businesses comply with food safety regulations?	Where might food safety risks arise in the food production chain?
when	When is food safety training mandatory for food handlers?	When did the food safety regulations first come into effect?	When can businesses expect routine inspections for food safety compliance?	When would consumers notice the benefits of stricter food safety laws?	When will updates to food safety regulations be announced?	When might a food handler need to renew their certification?
why	Why is food safety important for public health?	Why did the government feel the need to revise these regulations?	Why can maintaining food safety standards improve a company's reputation?	Why would governments prioritize funding for food safety education?	Why will stricter food safety laws protect vulnerable populations?	Why might businesses struggle to adapt to new food safety requirements?
how	How is compliance with food safety regulations monitored?	How did businesses adapt to new food safety requirements?	How can food safety regulations prevent foodborne illnesses?	How would proper food handling reduce contamination risks?	How will technology help monitor compliance with food safety standards?	How might businesses innovate to meet new food safety guidelines?

You can download a blank copy of the *Question Creation Table* in the appendices on page 195.

Connect: from page to practice

Looking through a specific unit of work and a student sample of the final summative task:

1. Identify the reading demands being asked of students throughout the unit.

2. Highlight which demands are currently being explicitly taught and scaffolded within the unit and which have the greatest complexity.

3. Highlight where and how you are checking for understanding during and after reading tasks.

4. Using a weaker student sample and your classroom experience, identify the aspects of the reading demands students generally struggle with the most.

5. Identify where these areas are being (or can be) supported within the unit and where they can also be extended. Connect specific support strategies and activities to these areas in your documentation.

Remember: While every teacher is collectively responsible for building reading capacity, it is up to you to explicitly teach and support the reading demands of the subject-specific reading required in your class.

Connecting reading... in summary

Reading skills
In order to read, a person needs to 'weave' together their understanding of background knowledge, vocabulary, language structures, verbal reasoning, literacy knowledge, and their phonological awareness, decoding and orthographic mapping skills to access different texts.

Reading demands
Teachers need to identify the reading demands they are placing on students in any subject. By considering the impact of the fixed and variable factors of any text, they can better identify the reading complexity and determine appropriate supports.

Assessing reading
Teachers need a variety of ways to check whether students have understood the reading demands of their subject. These can include: *spoken responses, processing organisers, summaries, quality note-making activities or any Check for Understanding task.*

The problem with reading
The problem with assessing how well a student has understood a text is that schools most often assess reading through writing tasks. This leaves the question whether the confusion is coming from the reading, or through an inability to articulate the understanding through the writing.

Reading difficulties
A gap or confusion in any isolated skill can cause reading issues, so teachers need strategies to support not just comprehension issues, but confusions at the word, sentence and text level.

Reading strategies
Different strategies can be used to support different reading difficulties.

#1 - decoding, PA and fluency issues
repeated, partnered or performance readings

#2 - vocabulary gaps and confusions
substitute and simplify

#3 - pronoun and connective confusions
connective match

#4 - literal comprehension issues
comprehension strategies (at word, sentence or text level

#5 - inference and interpretation building
ask questions to find answers

Connecting Whole-School Literacy in the Secondary Context

Chapter 4

Connecting writing

Key chapter concept: *Student difficulties in writing come from a variety of subskills that are further complicated due to the cognitive load required to balance so many complex skills simultaneously. Writing requires focus and energy, which is why it is such a powerful learning tool, but with so many competing factors, it is also one of the most difficult skills to teach.*

The skills to write

Writing is a phenomenally difficult, but powerfully important, life skill. It "requires the integration of multiple cognitive functions simultaneously: hand-eye coordination, language, memory, creativity, insight, logic, spatial intelligence and abstract thought" (Dean, 2019). Yet, balancing all these significant skills is only the beginning of the complexities schools face when attempting to teach students how to write across the curriculum.

In 2019, Joan Sedita took the concept of Scarborough's *Reading Rope* and created *The Writing Rope* (see Figure 4.0 overleaf). It expanded upon *The Simple View of Writing* (Berninger et al., 2002) by identifying the individual skills required for writing success. *The Writing Rope* has been adapted in semantic ways by other individuals, but conceptually, they all consider the key skills that must become more automatic (transcription skills) and more strategic (language processing skills) and how they work together to create skilled writing.

Figure 4.0: *The Writing Rope*

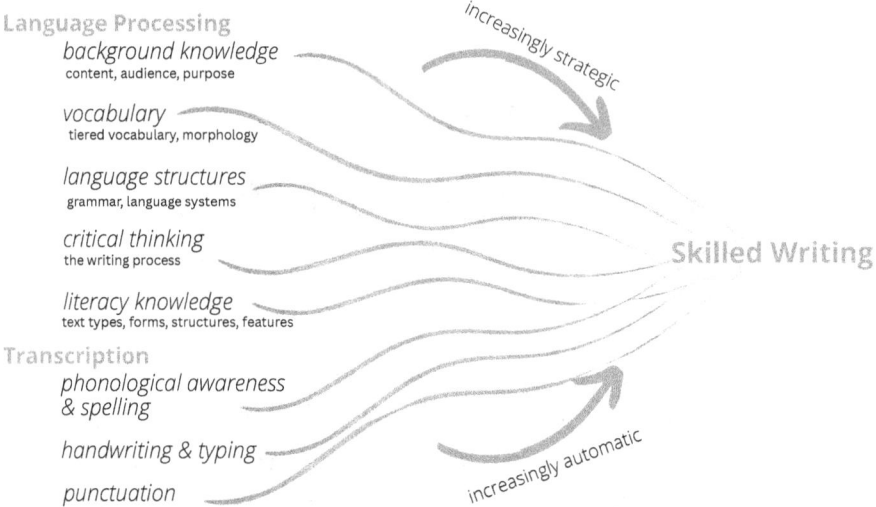

In 2006, Berninger and Winn revised *The Simple View of Writing* into *The Not-So-Simple View of Writing*. Acknowledging the vital place metacognition and working memory play in successful writing, they balanced the relationship between executive functioning skills and the original components of **transcription** (converting spoken language into the written form) and **language processing** (the ability to comprehend, produce and manipulate language) by representing the elements as interlocking pieces rather than a formula (as seen in Figure 4.1 opposite).

The importance placed on writing as a life skill, though, has been more recently called into question. The debate is initiated by teenagers who struggle with the effort and motivation required to improve their writing, but the deprioritising of the skill seems to solidify with the mainstream introduction of artificial intelligence (AI) as a way to brainstorm, draft, revise and edit any type of writing a person could desire. **So, why do we need to teach a student how to write if they can simply ask AI to do it for them?**

It is such perspectives that make it so important for teachers to understand *why* writing is so beneficial as a skill and the ways they can prioritise it as part of their students' learning in every class.

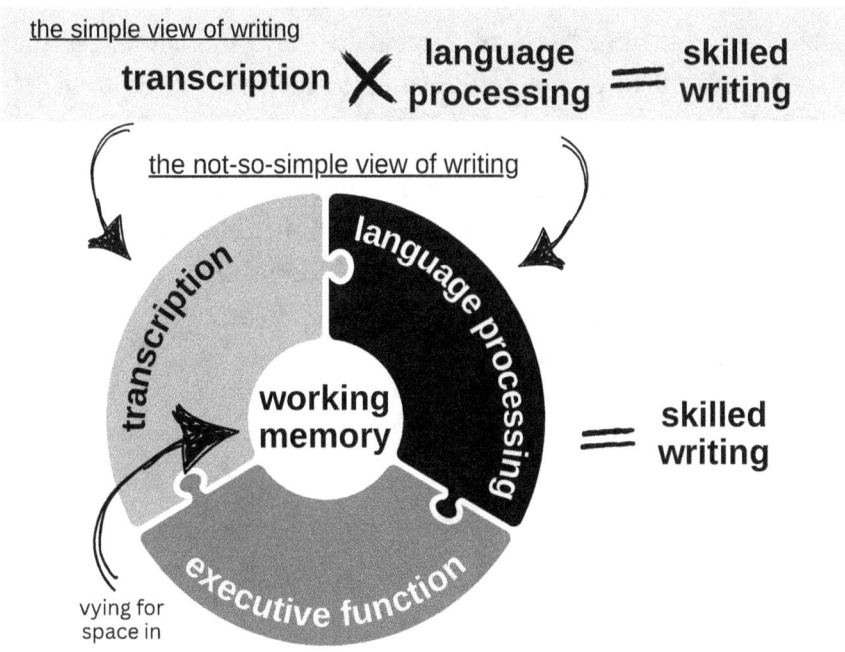

Figure 4.1: The Simple View of Writing and its transition into The Not-So-Simple View of Writing model

Willis (2011) writes in The Brain-Based Benefits of Writing for Math and Science Learning on Edutopia:

> "The practice of writing can enhance the brain's intake, processing, retaining, and retrieving of information. Through writing, students can increase their comfort with and success in understanding complex material, unfamiliar concepts and subject-specific vocabulary."

In other words, writing figuratively builds the brain's muscles, which can then be used literally to increase cognitive capacity.

But the benefits go further than this. Being able to translate thoughts into words on a page and understand how to shift writing for different audiences and purposes allows a person to navigate the complexities of life. The OECD (2019) reported 12.6% of Australians between the ages of 16 and 65 "score at the lowest levels of literacy", classifying them as illiterate. While there are no stand-alone national statistics on writing proficiency specifically, the Reading and Writing Hotline (2020) reported that "44% of Australians have literacy levels that make it difficult to complete the complex forms required to access essential services".

Learning how to write is not simply something that makes school easier, but as Quigley (2022) states, **"No statistic, however big, can capture the frustration and daily losses suffered by those people, and pupils, who struggle to write."** This is the reason that it becomes almost impossible to overemphasise the importance of writing as a skill.

> **QUESTIONS TO CONNECT**
> - What does 'skilled writing' look like in the context of your subject/s and class/es?
> - What specific writing skills do you notice students struggling with while writing in your class?
> - How confident are you to identify and support these individual skills?

Common writing gaps, confusions and areas for improvement

As seen in *The Writing Rope* (see Figure 4.0 on page 108), there are significant competing priorities that are vying for the limited attention available in a student's working memory at any one time. The following are some of the most common writing gaps, confusions and areas for improvement that are seen at varying degrees in every classroom.

For each of the five writing difficulties identified, some initial strategies have been included, along with an example of what this might look like in a secondary classroom.

1. Limited vocabulary

Chapter 2 explored why students are unable to express themselves explicitly or in more sophisticated ways if they do not have enough vocabulary to do so. When a student's active vocabulary is significantly less than their passive vocabulary, they will need to rely on their tier 1 vocabulary and attempt to intersperse this with some of the required tier 3 vocabulary that has explicitly been taught. This can often present itself as students 'writing the way they speak' or lacking the depth and sophistication to articulate their level of understanding of a concept – not necessarily because they do not understand, but often because they simply do not have the language to do so.

Supporting strategies:

- Activities in Chapter 2 emphasised the importance of exploring describing words alongside technical vocabulary and making the most of incidental vocabulary teaching opportunities. The focus of vocabulary teaching should always be on providing students with opportunities to *use* vocabulary by being able to spell the word when writing (and pronounce the word when speaking).
- Remember to provide students the opportunity to repeat and consolidate new words more than might seem required. It is difficult to predict how many exposures an individual might need before a new word is mapped to their long-term memory, so retrieval practice activities and opportunities to experiment and consolidate new vocabulary are vital.

- Additionally, if students don't *continue* to use the word, it can quickly convert back into their passive vocabulary. Consider maximising bell-ringers, *Activating Prior Knowledge* activities and exit slips along with providing ample speaking and writing opportunities with a focus on using new vocabulary (see the appendices on page 195).

Feedback example

> Question: Why is cybersecurity important?
> Cybersecurity is important because it stops hackers. If there isn't cybersecurity, people can lose their passwords. Cybersecurity also helps websites stay safe and protects data.
>
> This answers the question and shows your understanding of how cybersecurity is important. To maximise your marks in questions like this in the exam remember to use some of the technical language we have been using for this unit eg: **phishing, malware, ransomware, encryption, firewalls, multi-factor authentication.**
> Also, don't forget some descriptive language to show if things are positive or negative! eg: **essential, impenetrable, malicious, damaging.**

2. Punctuation errors

Many students forget the importance of **punctuation** (including capital letters) to clarify meaning, intonation and expression in a piece of writing, but punctuation helps a reader break a piece of writing into meaningful pieces and identify key terms, and supports the way readers can interpret appropriate tone and expression when inferring meaning from a text.

The skill of using punctuation is one that requires consolidation to the point of automaticity. Students shouldn't have to remember to use a capital letter when writing a person's name, place or starting a sentence; it should feel strange *not* to include one! Oftentimes, a student can clearly show understanding of when and where they should use capital letters, but when put under time pressure or asked to write a complex text, they suddenly 'forget' to use them. This is because they haven't automated the skill and when they are cognitively overloaded, something like punctuation gets 'lost' in the chaos.

Supporting strategies:

- Promote accurate use of punctuation (including capital letters) during *all* writing tasks – this includes informal tasks and drafts. **To automate the use of punctuation, students need to use punctuation *every* time they are writing.** This will require reminders and support, but explaining how much easier writing will become if they don't have to 'think' about punctuation provides students with evidence to justify the effort.

- Model and identify how to use punctuation when reading and writing for the class. Why is a capital letter used for that specific word? Why is a comma needed to separate those ideas? How can brackets or dashes be 'read'? Notice the use of a comma in the sentence frame provided, etc. Model how readers use punctuation to interpret writing and emphasise the need for writers to make it as easy as possible for their readers.

Feedback example

Question: Explain the impact of climate change on ecosystems.

climate change affects many ecosystems around the world scientist's say that greenhouse gases contribute to global warming which damages wildlife habitats. In places like in australia the great barrier reef is experiencing coral bleaching due to rising ocean temperatures. its important for countries to take action and reduce their carbon footprint before its too late.

This has some strong ideas and examples but needs to be more specific around the different 'impact' it has (you've only mentioned 'damaging wildlife habitats' and 'rising ocean temperatures').

Prioritise punctuation for readability:
- capital letters (for the start of sentences and proper nouns such as Australia),
- commas and full stops (to break ideas up for your reader)
- apostrophes (not needed for plurals – <u>scientists</u> – but needed for contractions it + is = <u>it's</u>).

3. Spelling errors

The importance of spelling seems to be decreasing as technology checks and supports the use of accurate spelling. A priority of clarity over accuracy when handwriting has also increased in many social and academic contexts. Yet, there is significant research emphasising how **improvements in spelling increase confidence, fluency, depth, sophistication and (obviously) accuracy in writing** (Moats, 2005; Reed, 2012) as well as the idea that spelling "unequivocally… matters for reading" (Gentry & Graham, 2010).

Yet, with the array of potential writing issues blocking a student's success, spelling can often seem the lowest priority for a teacher to focus their support on. This is particularly true for something that is "possibly one of the most 'unnatural' of skills we have to learn" (Adoniou, 2022). But when Adoniou reframes the skill in how "teaching spelling effectively can support reading and writing development", suddenly reprioritising the way we support spelling acquisition becomes significantly more relevant in the secondary context.

Similar to punctuation, if a student can reach a stage where they have automated the spelling of the words, then they don't have to draw from their limited working memory as they are writing. This begins with acknowledging the spelling alongside the meaning (and pronunciation) of any unfamiliar words – so the spelling of a new word is orthographically mapped into the long-term memory alongside its meaning – and continues with actively remapping familiar words that have been spelled incorrectly so many times that they now 'look normal' in their misspelled forms.

<u>Supporting strategies</u>:

- Rather than circle, underline or highlight a misspelled word, circle (underline or highlight) the *part* of the word the student has misspelled. Often, they have only misspelled a single letter, so drawing focus to that tiny element makes it significantly easier for the student to understand the error and recall it in future writing. The mindset of having spelled just a part of a word incorrectly, and not the whole word, can make the necessary revision seem significantly more achievable than having to memorise the entire word.

- Consider opportunities for students to explore the reason *why* a word is spelled the way it is and draw connections with other similarly spelled words. This could be due to the sound, meaning, rule or origin being used. Simply being given the time to investigate a word allows the spelling to connect to a deeper schema for the student. You can download the *Spelling Strategies* graphic, which supports students through a simple process to check and understand their spelling, in the appendices (page 195).

INEFFECTIVE SPELLING STRATEGIES

Generic spelling tests, routines such as *Look, Cover, Write, Check* or any repetitive rewriting of words are all <u>highly ineffective</u> ways to build spelling capacity.

They present the inaccurate idea that a person needs to <u>memorise</u> rather than <u>understand</u> new words, and they disconnect the meaningful parts of words from the letters used to spell them.

Traditional spelling tests also provide a generally misleading measure of spelling ability as they rely on short-term rather than long-term memory retention, and result in students still misspelling words when writing as the word becomes detached from the use of the word contextually.

Generic class spelling tests are also never able to tailor learning to the individual needs within a classroom. Students are being tested on words they already know how to spell; on words far beyond their spelling capabilities; or on words they are unlikely to ever use – therefore, the concept simply wastes everyone's time and energy!

- As discussed in *Going Beyond the Definition* (see page 53), always connect spelling (and pronunciation) to the meaning of any new words being explicitly taught. A student is much less likely to transfer this new word into their active vocabulary if they cannot spell it. This can be as simple as acknowledging the spelling when introducing a new vocabulary term.
- Build *Word Sums* (see page 63) and consider the **morphological** (meaning) level of the word or highlight the **orthographical** (spelling rules) or **etymological** (historical) reasons the word is spelled the way it is.

Classroom and feedback examples

When introducing new vocabulary, a teacher might say:

- "Notice the strange double vowel 'eu' at the start and the double 't' at the end of 'neurotransmitter.'"
- "Did you notice how the word 'position' is a key part of 'composition'? Com[position]. This might help us remember the meaning – and the spelling!"
- "There aren't many words that end in four vowels in a row, but 'onomatopoeia' is one of them. Honestly, the only way I can remember how to spell it is to sound it out like: on-o-mat-o-poe-i-a".

When providing feedback on student writing, a teacher might respond:

Question: Explain the process of photosynthesis.
Photosynthesis allows plants to convert sunlight into chemical energy, pr(e)ducing glucose, which fuels growth and development. `pro´ not `pre´ – because plants are `pro´ at `producing´!

4. Uncontrolled sentence structure

(fragmented sentences, overly long/short/grammatically incorrect sentences)

The more complex the text type, form and register, the more complex the sentence structures seem to become. Generally, these more academic or complex language features result in students struggling to control their ideas and expression – either within or across sentences – as the writing style becomes less familiar and further from their natural speech patterns.

The important consideration for teachers is whether students are struggling to control the text overall or if they are coming unstuck at the sentence level. If an entire piece of writing is confused, then the teacher should look at whether the student has controlled the individual paragraphs. If the paragraph is confused, then the teacher should look at whether the student has controlled the individual sentences.

Writing is built from words, into sentences, into paragraphs, into a text. Teachers can't hope to create great writers if we simply focus on how a student can write a full text.

If we focus on how to write good sentences, the outcome will be good texts.

Supporting strategies:

- **Sentence-Level Writing:** While building writing endurance and fluency is important, many concepts and writing skills can be more explicitly taught through writing sentences. Responding in full sentences allows students to practise articulating complex ideas without the overwhelm of controlling ideas across paragraphs and extended writing. Sentence responses can be excellent *Check for Understanding Activities* (see page 83) and are a length that teachers can provide individual feedback upon within the time constraints of a single period. See page 96 for more explicit sentence level activities.

- **Annotated Revisions:** Asking students to identify key elements of their writing can allow them to literally 'see' the pieces they are (or aren't) including and connecting. These annotations can be completed by the whole class, working with their own responses, and revisions made before submission. Examples include asking students to highlight the:
    - main subject of the sentence and any other references to the subject (are they being repetitive, unclear or are there opportunities for substitutions?)
    - analytical verb and the subject 'doing' the action
    - conjunction and draw arrows to the parts of the sentence the conjunction is connecting
    - verbs and check for consistency of tense
    - descriptive or explanatory words being used
    - first two words of every sentence (in a paragraph) and notice if the sentences are too long, too short, all start in the same way, don't include any connectives, etc.

    The important step with any guided revision is ensuring students have identified an area to focus on and have the time and capacity to revise, edit and receive feedback on their success.
- **Cohesive devices:** Often fractured sentences, or sentences that start to lose control, come from confusion around the cohesive devices being used. Has the student:
    - Used too many conjunctions?
    - Tried to connect too many pieces in one sentence?
    - Included a subordinating conjunction without adding it to an independent sentence?
    - Used a pronoun that makes it unclear what it is referencing?

    Asking students to highlight any cohesive devices (pronouns, conjunctions, substitutions, some adverbs, some determiners) and draw arrows back to the elements being referenced allows students to see how the pieces of their writing work (and connect!) together purposefully.

- **Performance Revisions:** Asking students to read their writing aloud can be a powerful way for many of them to hear the way their writing is not flowing or coming together. Performance revisions can make noticing a lack of punctuation easier to identify and can also help with overall flow and connection. Performance revisions can be completed in isolation but can also be successful with everyone in the class reading their drafts aloud at the same time – this way, no one feels embarrassed, and many find the moment of organised chaos enjoyable (except maybe the teacher with all the highly enthusiastic students!).

Feedback example

> Question: Explain how to find the slope of a line given two points (3, 5) and (7, 9)
> To find the slope subtract the y-values but subtract the x-values 9 minus 5 is 4 but 7 minus 3 is 4 and divide 4 by 4 to get 1 this is the slope.
>
> Your answer is mathematically correct, though your response makes it difficult for me to understand because you haven't used connectives correctly (or sentence barriers!) to explain the process.
>
> Think about using time markers (**firstly – then – finally**) to show the order of the steps to take.
> Also, be precise with how to show the relationship between concepts (subtract the y-values **AND THEN** subtract the x-values. 9 minus 5 is 5 **AND** 7 minus 3 is 4...sometimes the little words are just as important as the numbers!)

5. Illegible or messy handwriting

With the increase in technological writing tools, there has been an understandable increase in the illegibility and control of some students' handwriting. While there are people who argue that handwriting is less important as a life skill in contemporary society, there is significant research around its overwhelming benefits and importance.

People process things differently when they handwrite versus type. Wiley and Rapp (2021) conclusively found handwriting produces "faster learning and strengthening of representations" compared to "nonmotor practices" such as typing.

If a teacher wants a student to remember something, they will have a far greater chance of succeeding if the student handwrites the concepts than if they type or simply listen.

Clearer, more legible handwriting also leads to **increased writing confidence, expression and vocabulary**. Beyond making it significantly more pleasurable for teachers to read, focusing on improving student handwriting **"positively affects writing quality, length and fluency"** (McLean & Griffiths, 2024).

Yet, many teachers see focusing on handwriting in the secondary context as unnecessary or 'too late' to make a change. Doug (2019) would starkly disagree, arguing that "a handwriting policy should be a core priority for secondary schools" and "if educationalists want to raise pupils' literacy skills, they would be advised to focus their attention on handwriting as the linchpin of the schools' curriculum and pedagogical practices".

Supporting strategies:

- The first thing is to allow students to experiment with different types of pens. The thickness and shape of the shell and the type of tip and ink have significant impacts on handwriting legibility and should always be the starting point in attempting to improve handwriting skills in adolescent learners.

- Secondly, consider the student's seating position. Ideally, they will be seated with their feet flat on the floor and elbows comfortably resting at 90 degrees. While this is not always possible, recognising that handwriting comes from the movement of the elbow rather than the wrist can shift many students' understanding of how they write and how they can control their writing most effectively.
- Also, explore the impact of the angle of their paper. Depending on the slant of the writing, turning the paper diagonally one way or the other (or straight) also has a significant impact on the way writing presents itself on the page.
- Finally, focus on the area of greatest impact; is the handwriting issue to do with the:
  - *form* of specific letters
  - *size* of the letters
  - *space* between the letters/words
  - *position* of the letters on the line?

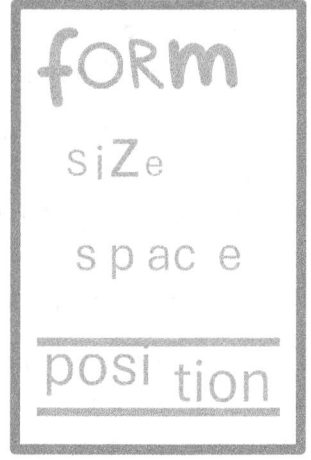

Any of these issues can be too small, big or inconsistent, but by focusing on something as specific as *'Your Ts when starting a word and your Ys when ending a word'* can become much less overwhelming and more realistic in achieving improvement for a student than simply asking them to 'watch' their handwriting or 'write neater'.

QUESTIONS TO CONNECT

- What skills do you most often see your students struggling with when writing different texts?
- What strategies do you (or can you) use to support them more specifically?
- Which strategies can be differentiated to support all learners, and which are needed to support your most struggling writers?
- Are these strategies explicitly taught, or rather suggested in feedback (either through discussions with individual students or in written feedback)?

Writing demands

There is a reason students' knowledge and understanding of content is most commonly assessed through writing in almost every subject area. It comes from the fact that writing is an effective tool for enhancing students' learning of content. Gentry and Graham (2010) emphasise how students' comprehension in any subject "improves when they write about what they read". Lehr, Osborn and Hiebert (2005) extend this concept by emphasising how "reading and writing are composing processes" that enable readers to organise and clarify their thinking. Given that "writing provides insight about literacy tools", students gain a deeper understanding of authorial choices when they write, which in turn supports more effective reading comprehension as a byproduct.

Many practical subjects initially assume that writing isn't the emphasis or priority in their course, but upon deeper reflection, students are required to engage in different forms of writing, for different audiences and purposes, throughout any given subject.

Sedita (2023) classifies these types of content writing into three categories:

1. **Quick Writes:** Low-stake, unrevised, ungraded, free writing
2. **Content Learning Tasks:** Focused learning, formative assessment-based writing
3. **Formal Writing Tasks:** Extended, revised, formally evaluated and graded writing.

Yet, the writing demands upon a student extend beyond these classifications even further. Articulating thoughts, opinions and understanding can occur in numerous text types and forms, and for different purposes and audiences. Table 4.0 includes a list of potential writing forms a student might be required to engage in across different subjects, contexts and situations. It is interesting to note the priority, value and support these different forms receive, and the opportunities students have to read authentic exemplar models as well as experiment, consolidate and refine their capacity to replicate them purposefully.

Table 4.0: Potential writing forms

essays	extended responses	reflective journals and learning logs	research projects
creative stories, comic strips	poetry, lyrics	scripts and dialogue	articles, opinion pieces, blogs
short answer responses	worksheets and handouts	graphic organisers	speeches, debates
instructions, recipes and procedural texts	reports, factsheets or pamphlets	brainstorming and planning documents	letters, emails, resumes, applications
posters, infographics	summaries, class notes	reviews, critiques	debates, advertisements

Once teachers have identified the writing demands being placed upon their students, they then need to consider the **writing complexity** to determine how best to support students in the writing task.

Similar to reading demands, the complexity of a text will depend on different potential factors that can be categorised as either fixed or variable.

Fixed factors are those the teacher (or context) has decided are the expectations of the writing. These include: • word length • text type and form • purpose and audience • register • time pressure • expected vocabulary.	**Variable factors** are those the student brings with them that can impact the way they engage with and ultimately create the text. These include: • background knowledge (of the content, text type, form and vocabulary) • motivation and confidence (their desire, perceived relevance of the writing and willingness to experiment) • automaticity of writing mechanics (spelling, punctuation, handwriting and syntactical awareness).

When determining the potential support for writing a given text, the teacher needs to consider the impact of both fixed and variable complexity factors. Depending on the elements with the highest impact, the most effective strategy for support will generally be different for each task. For example, an extended, multi-step research report is likely to require support from the research and planning stage all the way through to editing checklists and multiple stages of feedback. A short comprehension paragraph may only require an explanation of the expected length and content to include, and maybe peer reading to confirm the accuracy of the response.

Rather than see the list in Table 4.0 as an overwhelming array of structures and features to navigate, schools should notice the opportunities they have to prioritise, transfer, consolidate and extend student writing across the day. Imagine the impact on student writing if *every* teacher in a school expected students to write in full sentences (using a capital letter and a full stop) in *all* their responses, in *every* class across the day; or if teachers sent student emails back for revision before actioning if they were not properly structured, expressed or punctuated*.

If high expectations can be set alongside explicit instruction and support, then all students require is the time and consistent practice to consolidate and ultimately extend their writing skills more holistically.

> **QUESTIONS TO CONNECT**
>
> - What writing demands do you place on your students beyond the assessable tasks, and how complex are these demands?
> - Which writing tasks do you scaffold and explicitly teach, and which do you assume students should be able to construct independently?
> - What type of writing contexts do your students generally find the most difficult? How do you currently support these tasks?

---

* I do this every year – initially, I set up the expectations and features of an email and explain how written communication is more formal than speech. Then, if I get an email that includes no subject line or just attaches a document without anything else in the email, I reply with: **'This email does not conform to the expected structures and features of the text type. Any requests will only be actioned after a revised response is sent. Thank you in advance for your commitment to learning social etiquette.'** Interestingly, I've had many students thank me for teaching them how to construct an email properly!

The writing process

The concept of the writing process was first studied and formalised by researchers Linda Flower and John R Hayes in the 1980s. While innumerable acronyms and variations in the language have been used across the decades, the concept, in principle, remains the same.

In order to write successfully, a person has to initially *think*. This might include brainstorming, researching, interviewing, reading and/or planning, but someone can't write if they don't know what they are going to write about. The person then needs to *draft* the writing and work through any number of opportunities to *revise* and *edit* the writing for clarity, accuracy and effect. This may happen in the moment by monitoring as they write, or it might come after writing, by re-reading the piece in its entirety and using checklists, criteria or feedback to inform ways to revise and edit purposefully.

Figure 4.2: The essential elements of the writing process

prewriting → drafting → revising → editing
research
brainstorming
planning

While the processes of pre- and post-writing are always essentially the same in principle, they can look very different depending on the type of writing. A person thinks, drafts and edits a text message in a very different way than if they were writing a job application. Yet, they would still need to consider what they were going to write before they started drafting the message (prewriting), consider the appropriate language and features for the specific audience and purpose while writing (drafting), and then spend a moment re-reading the message to check for clarity, effectiveness and accuracy (revising/editing). While much of this might occur very quickly or even subconsciously, the process remains consistent (and we acknowledge how confusing that friend is who forgets to re-read their message before sending!).

Table 4.1: Comparing the expectations of the writing process for different text forms

	Essay	Short answer response	Research project
Prewriting	Requires prior learning, collation and categorisation; planning templates often are significantly detailed	Minimal brainstorming and planning, often completed by simply annotating the question	Requires research and understanding the elements of the task; planning often involves categorising material or sequencing processes
Drafting	Conscious referral to the plan throughout; drafting in paragraphs	Written in one moment, often in a single process	Often written over an extended period – in conjunction with the sequenced actions in the plan
Revising	Often revised at the paragraph level for wording and the whole text for the overall response	Revising often combined with editing in one quick re-read to ensure the key elements of the question have been answered	Revising often occurs throughout the drafting; then the cumulation of the material once complete
Editing	Final read to check for accurate spelling, punctuation and grammatical errors		Final editing for accuracy and clarity often comes with the final publishing processes

You can download a copy of the *Writing Process Expectations* table in the appendices on page 195.

Having a variety of strategies to draw from at each stage of the writing process allows students to access the expectations of each task in realistic and purposeful ways.

Different strategies will be more effective for different writing tasks and conditions, but if teachers across the school can draw from similar strategies, or use common language around options and approaches, students are more likely to transfer and build the capacity they have around these important skills. Table 4.2 identifies several potential strategies across the different stages of the writing process.

Table 4.2: Potential strategies for each stage of the writing process

Brainstorming	• Don't restrict yourself to good ideas • Categorise as you brainstorm and then synthesise afterwards • Get ideas down and allow yourself to adapt in the planning stage • It only has to make sense to you – dot points, shorthand, visuals, alternative language, etc. are all appropriate during brainstorming
Planning	• Practise backwards planning* to know what you need from your plan • Focus on sequencing and including all the elements • Know your strengths and areas for improvement, and plan to support both • Check your plan against the criteria • Your plan only has to make sense to you – don't worry about writing full sentences or explaining yourself here
Drafting	• Go back and check your plan regularly • Go back and add to your plan as you are writing, if needed • Don't get stuck on a word – trust the revision process and keep moving • Keep monitoring for meaning; re-read the sentence before adding the next

---

* **Backwards planning** involves using a completed worked example and determining what the plan for the response 'would' have been. This shows students what an effective plan can look like and not only what details are important, but how they are then transferred into the writing task. Students then have the option of using the plan to construct their own response, which emphasises that even the same information can be presented in many ways and for different impact and effect.

Revising	• Have different strategies for revising (and editing) in the moment and after drafting • Consider ARMS – add, remove, move, substitute • Check your draft against the criteria • Check and potentially change – narrative structure, perspective, tense, formatting, register, language, modality • Give yourself as much space and time as possible between the draft and the revisions (it is difficult to notice errors if we read straight after writing) • Read for *meaning*
Editing	• Read the text backwards to focus on words rather than meaning • Check CUPS – capitalisation, usage (grammar), punctuation, spelling • Check handwriting legibility • Performance editing – read your work aloud as it 'sounds' in your head and notice punctuation and expression • Read for *accuracy*

You can download a copy of the *Strategies Across the Writing Process* table in the appendices on page 195.

QUESTIONS TO CONNECT

- What does the writing process look like for the writing tasks in your classes?
- How does the writing process look different for the different tasks you have?
- How do you currently support and extend students through the writing process in different tasks?

Writing activities for every classroom

There are innumerable ways a teacher can explicitly teach, experiment or extend writing skills in their classroom. The first step is to ensure students are writing in every lesson – not just words, but full sentences. Then, rather than adding an explicit focus on writing, teachers can draw from a variety of writing strategies and activities that can be used in different contexts to support student understanding alongside building writing development.

The following five activities can be used in any classroom and for any content in various ways depending on need, ability, set-up and time available.

1. Sentence Starters and Additions

Providing students with the opportunity to write quality sentences every lesson is one of the easiest and most effective writing strategies a school can adopt. Alex Quigley, in his book *Closing the Writing Gap* (2022), reiterates how "practising one sentence brilliantly may be worth more than writing out a hundred of them in haste" and elaborates on four key sentence variation strategies:

- **Sentence Combining** – revising two or more sentences into one
- **Sentence Shrinking** – revising a long sentence into a more succinct, clear one
- **Sentence Expanding** – revising a simple statement by adding words, phrases or clauses to construct a detailed sentence
- **Sentence Signposting** (also known as *Sentence Framing*) – completing a sentence after being given a starting word, phrase or dependent clause.

One of these potential signposts could be a **fronted adverbial** (an adverb that begins a sentence). Adverbs are the most flexible word class in that they can move to almost any position in a sentence. They can also modify not only verbs, but adjectives, other adverbs and whole clauses. Spoken syntax rarely uses adverbs to modify clauses, so students are less likely to see this as an option or can find that this sentence structure initially feels strange.

Instructions:
- Provide students with a sentence and ask them to choose an appropriate adverb (for example, respectfully, historically, gradually) to either start or include somewhere in the sentence.
- Provide an adverb or adverbial phrase and ask students to complete the sentence regarding the topic of study.

Classroom example

> **Task**: Complete the following sentences, demonstrating your understanding of our unit on Indigenous studies:
>
> eg: **With deep respect for the land**...*Indigenous communities uphold their traditions and connection to nature.*
>
> 1. In the early colonial period *Indigenous communities were forced off their land, but many found ways to protect their culture.*
> 2. Across generations *elders have passed down important knowledge about language, land care and traditions.*
> 3. Before the arrival of Europeans *Indigenous nations had complex societies with laws, leaders and ways of caring for Country.*
> 4. By practising sustainable hunting and farming *they were able to care for animals and plants without harming the ecosystem.*
> 5. After centuries of displacement *many Indigenous communities are still working to reclaim land, rights and recognition.*

Appositives are a way that students can expand simple sentences. These are essentially extended pronoun phrases (phrases that can replace a noun) that are added directly *after* the noun they are referring to and provide further information in a succinct and formal way. Because they are considered 'non-essential information', they need to be bracketed with commas. Again, they are rarely used in spoken language but are a simple way for students to add detail and formality to their writing.

Instructions:

Ask students to brainstorm ways they might explain or describe a specific concept (noun) and consider how differently the concept is perceived depending on how it is described.

For example: 1950s Australia...

- a young federation still shaping its national identity...
- a nation under Menzies' conservative leadership...
- a society steeped in Anglo-centric values...
- a land of backyard cricket and gendered domesticity...

Students can then write a sentence about the concept including an appositive of their choice or can be provided with a sentence and revise it by adding different appositives for effect.

Classroom example

> **Task:** Revise the following sentences by adding an appositive to demonstrate your understanding of the key concept being described.
>
> eg: **Fractions, a way to represent parts of a whole, are foundational in understanding rations and proportions.**
>
> The Pythagorean theorem ^ is essential in geometry.
> *a formula of the length of a triangle's sides,*
>
> Probability ^ is calculated by dividing favourable by total outcomes.
> *the chance of something happening*
>
> Quadratic equations ^ often have two solutions.
> *an expression that forms a curve when graphed,*
>
> An acute angle ^ is common in many geometric figures.
> *an angle under 90°,*
>
> Integers ^ are used in numerous real-world contexts.
> *positive or negative numbers, or zero,*

Experimenting with and building complex sentences extends students to connect multiple ideas within a single sentence. This requires students to be working with **independent and dependent sentences** (or clauses if we are being technical). A sentence is classified as *independent* if it can stand alone as a grammatically complete sentence. A *dependent* sentence includes a **subordinate conjunction***, which means it must connect with an independent clause for it to make sense and be grammatically correct.

Instructions:

- Give students two sentences and ask them to blend them into one by choosing an appropriate conjunction to show the relationship between sentences.
- Give students an independent clause and a conjunction, and ask them to finish the sentence, or a dependent clause and ask them to add an independent clause.

Classroom example

Task: Complete the following sentences by adding an appropriate independent clause to the end of these dependent clauses.

eg: *When the tempo of a piece increases...listeners may feel a heightened emotional response, like excitement or tension.*

1. If a composition uses dissonance, *the mood of the piece often shifts towards something darker or more dramatic.*
2. Before the orchestra repeats the main motif, *a solo instrument might introduce a variation to build anticipation.*
3. While the rhythm alternates between triple and duple meter, *the listener may feel a sense of unpredictability or surprise.*
4. Since the key modulates from major to minor, *the emotional tone shifts to add contrast and depth.*
5. As the time signature changes mid-piece, *the feeling and pacing of the music are suddenly transformed.*

---

* A **subordinate conjunction** is a word that shows a relationship, for example, while, since, as.

2. Cohesive ties

Any word that refers back to a previous word is classified as a **cohesive tie**. The most recognised is the pronoun, but cohesive ties can also be substitutions (synonyms, or phrases like appositives), repetitions and omissions. Cohesive ties create flow and coherence in writing and help readers make sense of a text. Many writers will struggle to control or extend their cohesive tie use, so focusing on them supports more sophisticated ways into the content.

Instructions:

- Provide several sentences that simply repeat the main subject every time. Ask students to revise the writing to consider ways to say the subject without being repetitive or restructure the sentences for better flow.
- Ask students to write a sentence or revise their writing by considering different ways they can identify, describe and connect the main subject throughout.

Classroom example

Task: Highlight all the repetitions occurring in the following paragraph and then revise the paragraph to provide flow, more detail and less repetition.

The mortise and tenon joint is a traditional method of joining two pieces of wood. The mortise and tenon joint has strength and simplicity. The mortise and tenon joint involves crafting a rectangular 'tenon' on one piece of wood to fit snugly into a matching 'mortise' cut into another piece of wood. Although the mortise and tenon joint requires precision, skilled woodworkers often rely on the mortise and tenon joint for structural integrity and aesthetic appeal, making the mortise and tenon joint a popular choice in furniture making.

Your revision

The mortise and tenon joint, a traditional method of joining two pieces of wood, is used for its strength and simplicity. It involves crafting a rectangular 'tenon' on one piece of wood to fit snugly into a matching 'mortise' cut into another. Although the technique requires precision, skilled woodworkers often rely on this joint for structural integrity and aesthetic appeal, making it a popular choice in furniture making.

---

3. Guided revisions

This is a process where the teacher facilitates a whole-class revision by guiding students through identifying and *Annotating* (see page 90) different elements in their own writing draft. This process is a natural differentiation activity, as every student is working on a text they have drafted themselves, and works to encourage independent revision while emphasising critical elements that will impact the success of the task.

Key elements commonly considered in many tasks include:

- key elements of the criteria
- specific connections to the question or task
- analytical, reflective, evaluative, etc. specific vocabulary
- technical language (and how it should be used)
- examples, evidence or specific elements

- sentence number or length
- structural features included, for example, subheadings, visuals
- connectives, conjunctions or specific relationships between elements.

Once the elements have been highlighted, students can 'see' gaps or areas for revision. The bonus of this visual approach means teachers can also easily see common problem areas across a class that may require more explicit instruction or support.

Classroom example

> Reading through your response to question three, can you please underline the first two words in every sentence? Just draw a line under the first two words.
>
> Once you've done that: what do you notice? How many sentences have you written? Do you have one or two really long sentences, or lots of little sentences? Do your sentences start with a capital letter and end in a full stop? Will you need to revise your sentences? If so, write 'sentences' at the side to come back to.
>
> Now, with a highlighter or different-coloured pen, can you please circle the word 'belief' in the question and then go through your response and circle any time you have used the word 'belief' or another word that means belief? That might be a pronoun such as 'it' or 'that', but it could also be something like 'believes', 'opinion' or 'perspective'. Any time you've referred to the element of 'belief'.
>
> Once you have done that, what do you notice? How many times have you referred to it? Have you only mentioned it at the start and/or the end of your answer? Or are you being overly repetitive? Will you need to revise your response, so it more clearly connects with 'belief'? If so, write 'belief' at the side to come back to later.

4. Gallery Walks

There is great benefit for students to be able to read and engage with each other's writing, though peer assessment can be fraught with complexities and inconsistent results. A *Gallery Walk* involves students displaying their writing on the walls (or simply placing it around the room) and allowing time for the students to move between pieces, reading and leaving comments on the work. These comments can be reflections, questions or suggestions for improvement. The bonus of this style of collaborative feedback is that the teacher can also move around the room, ensuring the highest level of feedback is offered, and students have access to numerous responses, as well as the feedback being provided along the way.

Explicit teaching, with sentence starter examples, may need to occur prior to students undertaking a *Gallery Walk* for the first time, particularly around ways to effectively provide feedback, respecting other student writing and the benefits for both the writer and the person providing feedback.

Many of the sentence frames from the *Accountable Talk* on page 26 may be useful starting points for supporting the language around providing feedback.

Gallery Walks can be implemented in numerous ways including:
- Feedback being offered by placing a sticky note onto the writing or being added to a 'feedback form' placed next to the writing
- Students being given a checklist of elements to identify and potentially respond to (see Classroom example opposite)
- Different groups of students being given specific elements to focus on as 'experts' in their feedback
- Writing can be de-identified so that students are responding to the writing rather than the individual
- Writing can be worked examples where students are asked to identify features that work well, or don't respond to the task, before drafting or revising their own.

Classroom example

CIVICS PROPOSAL GALLERY WALK

As you read your classmates' proposals, use this table to guide your feedback.

ELEMENT	WHAT TO LOOK FOR	POTENTIAL FEEDBACK
Community issue and improvement proposal	Is the issue clearly stated? Is the solution actionable?	• Your proposal feels achievable because… • To make the issue clearer, you could… • I'm wondering how this issue affects…
Persuasive explanation of why the issue matters	Does the proposal explain why the issue matters?	• It is clear this issue matters because… • You might strengthen your explanation by… • What would happen if this problem was…
Evidence to support the proposal	Are there supporting details? Are they relevant / effective?	• Your example helps support your idea by… • You could improve your evidence by… • I'm not sure how the example connects to…
Consideration of perspectives or stakeholders	Are different community members considered?	• It is thoughtful that you included… • Have you considered the opinion of… • What challenges might your idea face from…
Logical structure and paragraphing	Does the information flow naturally? Using logical paragraphs?	• Your structure helps the reader because… • You could make your paragraphs clearer by… • A linking sentence might help connect…
Use of formal and persuasive language	Is the writing clear, formal and persuasive?	• Your proposal sounds confident most when… • To sound more formal, you could replace… • Would a stronger verb be more persuasive…
Clear call to action or conclusion	Is there a clear next step and conclusion?	• Your conclusion leaves a strong impression by… • Your call to action could be more direct by… • What should the reader do after reading?

As you read the proposals, jot down any techniques, ideas or features you might like to use in your own revision.

- Use the community name more regularly throughout
- Give an example at each stage of the proposal
- 'community-minded' - 'future-focused' - 'for the benefit of all'

You can download a blank copy of the *Gallery Walk* handout in the appendices on page 195.

5. Writing Templates

There are innumerable examples of templates to assist students to think and process before writing, and to scaffold writing during drafting. Many of these can be easily downloaded, but often the most effective *Writing Templates* are the ones created for specific writing tasks.

Elements to consider when designing, choosing or using *Writing Templates* include:

- Ensure templates work the way students need them to support their writing, rather than feel restricted by the way an organiser 'should' look or the space it normally provides.
- Templates can be scaffolded by pre-filling certain elements for some students or adding space or additional elements for extension.
- Ensure there is ample space for students to write their responses depending on the expectations of the task.
- Consider how students can label and annotate their templates to 'check' if they have responded to the criteria or have included all expected elements.
- The principle of backwards planning (see page 129) can be applied to any *Writing Template*, where a final writing sample is explored and students then decide what the relevant template would have looked like for the piece.
- Don't assume students can jump from a planning or brainstorming document directly to writing – many students need help to scaffold from the prewriting templates to the drafting as well.
- Support students in the way they can *use* any prewriting templates when drafting – how often or when to refer to the planning; ways to 'check off' or connect from the plan into the writing; even where the planning page can most effectively be placed while writing!

See the appendices on page 195 for a *Selection of Writing Organisers*.

Connect: from page to practice

Looking through a specific unit of work and a student sample of the final summative task:

1. Identify the writing demands being asked of students throughout the unit.

2. Highlight which demands are currently being explicitly taught and scaffolded within the unit and which have the greatest complexity.

3. Using a weaker student sample and your teacher experience, identify the aspects of the writing demands students generally struggle with the most.

4. Identify where these areas are being (or can be) supported within the unit and where they can also be extended and then connect specific strategies and activities to these areas in your documentation.

Remember: While every teacher is building writing skills collectively, it is up to you to teach the subject-specific writing skills your class requires.

Connecting writing... in summary

Writing skills
In order to write, a person needs to 'weave' together their background knowledge, vocabulary, understanding of language structures, critical thinking skills and literacy knowledge, while employing their skills of spelling, punctuation and handwriting.

Writing difficulties
A gap or confusion in any isolated skill can cause writing issues, so teachers need strategies to support a variety of writing issues as well as extend abilities of expression, clarity, accuracy and increasing sophistication.

Writing demands
Teachers need to identify the writing demands they place on students. Each task brings both fixed and variable complexities as students must navigate the structures and features of the text type and form, as well as the specialised vocabulary, purposes and contexts of the writing.

The problem with writing
As a skill, writing is a significantly more difficult task than reading. Students have to balance so many competing factors that their limited working memory and executive functioning skills can often be completely overwhelmed. This is why working towards automating mechanical elements (spelling, handwriting, punctuation) are initially vital.

The benefits of writing
Writing maximises the way students can process reading and conceptual understanding and transfer this learning into their long-term memory. Writing helps a student to learn: particularly if it is handwritten!

Writing activities
Different writing activities can be used to process new content and support students through the stages of the writing process, including:
1. Sentence Starters and Additions
2. Cohesive Ties
3. Guided Revisions
4. Gallery Walks
5. Writing Templates

The writing process
Each writing task will require students to approach the stages of the writing process slightly differently. Due to this, teachers should consider different strategies to support students through the prewriting (brainstorming, research and planning), drafting, revising and editing stages of any writing task.

Connecting Whole-School Literacy in the Secondary Context

Chapter 5
Leading whole-school literacy

Key chapter concept: *Leading literacy development in any context is a balancing act of multilayered complexity. Developing a Literacy Framework and Action Plan is an effective way to mitigate the competing priorities and significant number of skills required to build staff capacity in ways to then develop literacy skills for all students. The process not only lays the foundations for schools to begin or build upon their literacy initiatives but also provides a clear direction that ensures the focus is sustainable, achievable and ultimately effective.*

Why leading literacy never ends

As a leader, you understand better than anyone how the greatest skill your school can offer its students is the ability to read and comprehend as well as to write and articulate their understanding and opinions. No matter the school or subject you teach, it is your responsibility to promote the reality that literacy significantly impacts student success, academically and in life.

Beyond improving the entire results of your school, it is (surely) a moral obligation that students leave Year 12 with the literacy skills to navigate life (if not future academic pursuits). Literacy in this sense becomes the door for students' future opportunities and success.

Tam (2017) exposes how the effects of poor literacy beyond the school years include "emotional, social and financial burdens", while those with the lowest level of education have a statistically reduced life expectancy of up to nine years compared to those with the highest levels (Welsh et al., 2021).

Literacy is the gateway for students to access the content of each subject and articulate their understanding. It then becomes your focus to ensure the skills of reading and writing (as illustrated in the *Reading* and *Writing Ropes*) continue to increase in sophistication and automaticity as individuals extend their capacity to read and write. Every individual is constantly improving their literacy skills throughout their life, but it is rarely as important, or more of an opportunity, than during school.

Maximising this opportunity to increase lifelong literacy skills throughout the school years, therefore, should become a key priority for any school.

Taking all this into consideration, any literacy professional development and whole-school literacy focus must be more than simply another goal in your school's Annual Improvement Plan, or a tokenistic percentage to increase in the school's Strategic Plan. Instead, a focus on literacy must be embedded into the school culture and into the school's professional development calendar purposefully and continuously.

Initially, this focus will require planning, effort, resourcing and prioritising, but once established, it should then simply become another part of the fabric of the school, where the curriculum and pedagogies for continual literacy improvement are understood, respected and actioned daily from both staff and students alike.

QUESTIONS TO CONNECT

- Where does literacy currently sit in the culture of your school?
- In what ways has your school engaged with and responded to literacy professional development in the past?
- Where does literacy sit as a priority and focus for the leadership and within the school calendar?

The complexity of focusing on literacy and building staff capacity

The reality of embedding literacy as a priority; building staff literacy knowledge and teaching capacity; and developing a school-wide culture around literacy is far from a simple one-and-done workshop, program or approach. Understanding the complexities of beginning (and maintaining!) such a focus needs to be acknowledged and considered before any planning and implementation can, or should, take place.

The complexities in focusing on literacy and building staff knowledge, experience and efficacy with the literacy demands of their subject and year level fall into three main categories:

1. The overwhelming number of elements that need to be considered and balanced in the teaching and learning of literacy, and the time it takes to upskill staff to process and apply that amount of information.
2. The significant diversity of student literacy skills and knowledge in any class or year level, and the individual strategies to best support and capitalise on their development.
3. The significant diversity of teacher literacy skills, knowledge, confidence and experience in teaching and supporting these

skills, along with the complexity of building collective efficacy in a varied and potentially transient team.

1. The number of elements and the limited time

As explored throughout this text, there are so many individual elements to literacy within vocabulary, reading and writing. So, for your school to consider staff professional development, it can seem like you have to: be superficial at best; spend significant time covering every element to the detriment of all other priorities; or simply select a few key elements but never connect everything together.

Other competing priorities in the school calendar also need to be given time and focus, so finding time in a packed school calendar can be challenging, and trying to explicitly teach and inspire staff during an after-school mandatory meeting rarely results in quality literacy professional development.

Essentially, there is too much to do and not enough time to do it!

2. The diversity of student skills

Students arrive at school with an array of: language skills, background and knowledge; language understandings; language disorders; physical limitations; motivations; and support. Understanding that by the time students reach high school there can be anywhere up to eight or more years' difference in literacy skill levels in any one class means teachers are being asked to navigate how to explicitly teach, scaffold, consolidate and extend content and learning simultaneously.

While an awareness of this need for differentiation is critical, the overwhelm in how to support all these students individually, within the context of teaching a mandated and consistent curriculum, means teachers are often fighting between what individual students need and what the class is required to achieve collectively.

When literacy is then 'added' to the demands of a teacher as a school focus, it can seem not only unfair and unrealistic, but like a distracting focus from the subject-specific content and skills teachers are already struggling to find the time and capacity to teach.

The important factor to remember with any literacy professional development or implementation, therefore, is that literacy should never be 'added' or seen as 'other' to the content and skills being taught in any subject (other than English!) but rather:

Literacy professional development should focus on how to support, consolidate and extend the content knowledge and skills of a subject *through* literacy.

While this focus might initially seem semantic, it is critical not only to the longevity and uptake of the initiative, but also the success and effectiveness of the focus overall. By acknowledging the reading and writing demands within their subject, a teacher (of any subject) can consider the strategies and language they can use to better support and extend a student to a deeper understanding of the content. The incidental consequence just happens to be that students can then transfer and develop their literacy skills holistically, while the cognitive load prioritises the subject-specific learning.

3. The diversity of teacher skills

Just as students arrive with an array of skills, knowledge and experience, so do the teaching staff of your school. In any given year, your teaching cohort is likely to be made up of any mixture of:

- experienced teachers who have been at the school for an extended time
- experienced teachers new to the school
- leading teachers with competing administrative priorities
- graduate or early-career teachers
- permission-to-teach teachers
- teacher librarians
- specialist teachers working across different schools

- long-term casual relief teachers
- educational support staff
- teachers teaching out-of-field.

Within any of these classifications, individuals bring their own skills, understandings and perspectives to their teaching and their own learning. They may have been taught or worked in a setting that believed in contradicting pedagogical beliefs; have never been exposed to the specific language and approaches being emphasised at your school; or be an ex-literacy professor with 20 years' experience. You also need to consider staff turnover, making it increasingly difficult to build capacity from one year to the next.

In this way, navigating professional development for your staff needs to be just as differentiated (if not more) than teaching needs to be in the classroom.

All this might be why you have been feeling overwhelmed, frustrated or at a loss as to how making any real change is even possible! Acknowledging the complexities is the first step – there is no point pretending reality is something it is not. Then, take a breath and read on to learn how your school *can* combat these blockers most effectively.

QUESTIONS TO CONNECT

- What are the main complexities and blockers you are facing when considering ways to implement and action professional development and building staff literacy capacity at your school?
- How well do you know the literacy skills and knowledge of the students and staff at your school?
- How confident are you currently feeling about leading literacy in the context of your school?

The Literacy Framework

A model for building consistency, longevity and the accumulation of literacy skills.

The concept of a *Whole-School Literacy Framework (WSLF)* came from the desire to work *with* the complexities of a school's system rather than against them. It came from wanting to continue to build staff capacity, when they were ready, and find an approach that could maximise consistency as well as longevity when staff turnover and competing priorities make professional development feel like they always have to start from scratch. Finally, the design was intended to allow schools to dive into one element of literacy (while acknowledging it as only one piece of the complex puzzle that is literacy more generally) and allow schools to engage with new information and strategies without losing prior learning, resources and effort.

Essentially, the *WSLF* is a visual representation accentuating all the key elements of literacy and the relationships between them, while connecting any other school priorities such as teaching and learning models, explicit instructional models, curriculum designs, differentiation approaches and/or behaviour processes already (or soon to be) implemented.

The idea is that staff can see how a specific element of literacy being focused upon connects within the wider teaching and learning expectations of the school. The benefit of the visual allows leaders to 'zoom into' a specific category for professional development and 'zoom out' to see how that concept is only one part of the wider understanding of literacy and teaching.

Often, professional development can feel immediate, and teachers might go and implement a strategy the next day. But then another workshop comes along and the original strategy moves to the background to be replaced by something else. The *WSLF* is designed to balance the literacy focus across the classroom, curriculum and school calendar without competing against other priorities, but working alongside and with them.

The following school models reveal the extent to which the *WSLF* varies depending on each unique context.

Figure 5.0: *WSLF* School Example #1 – The Layers of Literacy

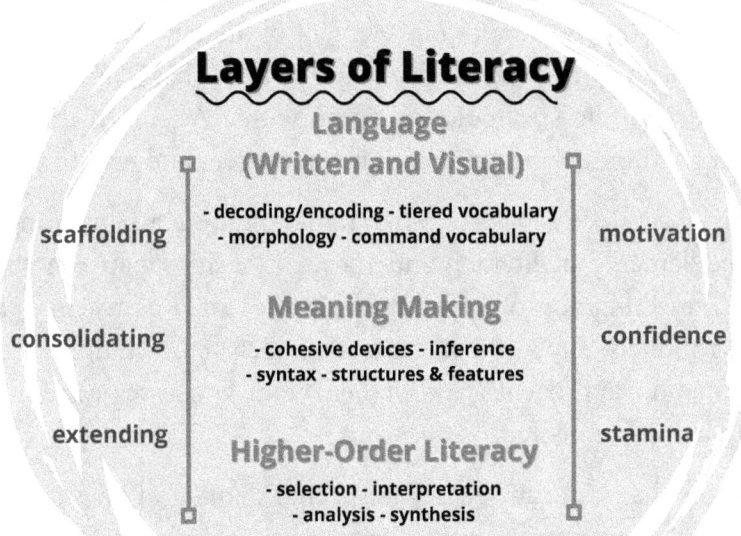

In this *Layers of Literacy* example, a city girls' school wanted to connect the key elements of literacy with not only the increasing differentiation required in their classrooms, but the social-emotional skills often impacting student success. They had a clear vision to find success in literacy (rather than simply improve the data) and allowed themselves realistic time to focus professional development on one 'Layer' per year, cumulatively building staff capacity over three years before working more holistically across the Framework. While they ran Whole-Staff Professional Development once a term during an after-school staff meeting, most of the work was explored and consolidated in Learning Area teams.

Figure 5.1: *WSLF* School Example #2 – The Literacy Arc

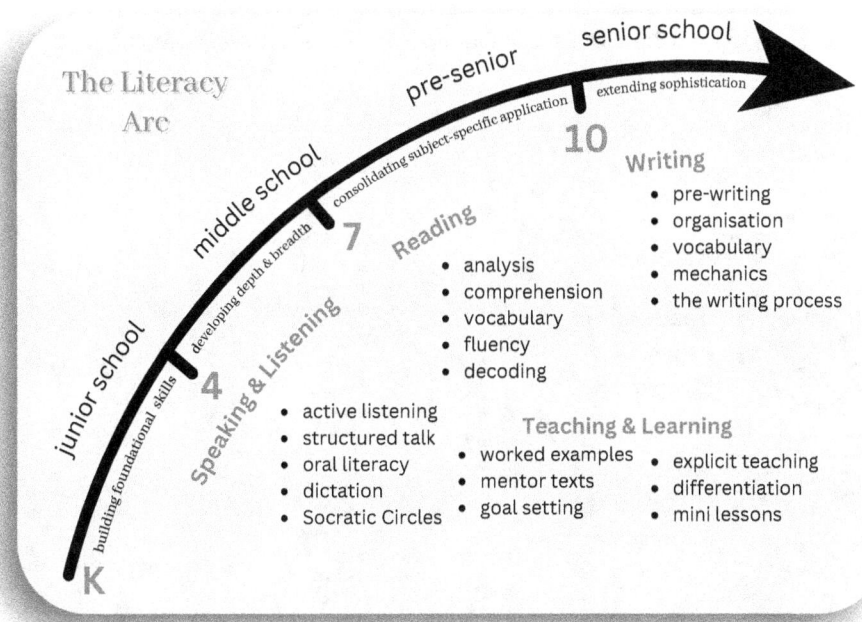

In this *Literacy Arc* example, a K–12 coeducational grammar school wanted to bridge the gap between the sub-schools across the same campus. By connecting the similarities in literacy skills and language but acknowledging the different foci and expectations in literacy instruction across the year levels, the school was able to use the 'Arc' to begin to cement a consistent language and approach to literacy understanding and development across a student's journey through the school.

Initially, much of the planning and work happened with the sub-school leaders, before time and support came through Professional Learning Community (PLC) groups as a way to consolidate the Whole-Staff Curriculum Day Professional Development that occurred once a semester. Future goals will be to use the 'Arc' to connect with a new explicit instructional model being introduced and continue embedding literacy strategies while updating curriculum documentation.

Figure 5.2: *WSLF* School Example #3 – The Literacy Branch

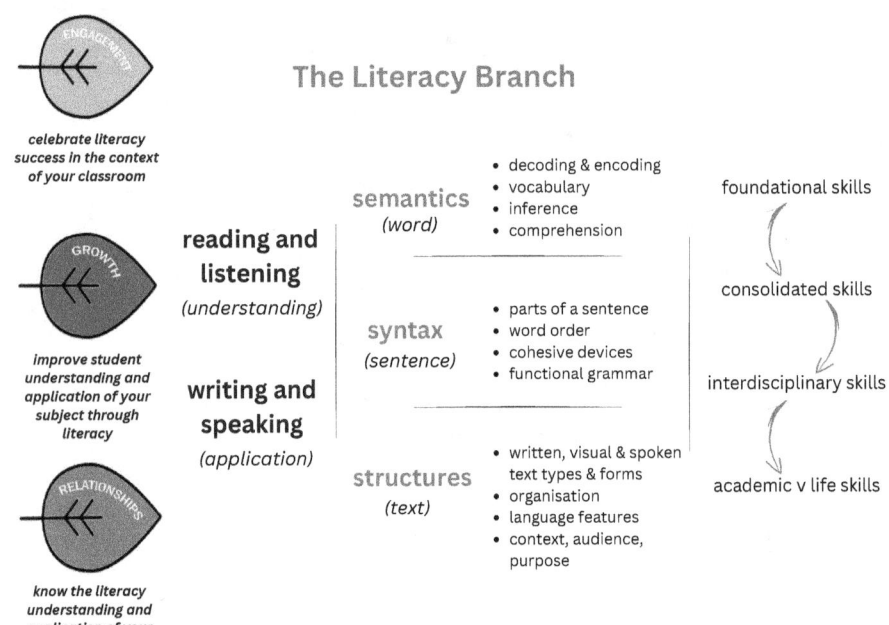

In this *Literacy Branch* example, a regional P–12 government school had built a clear teaching and learning model with 'leaves' representing the different areas of focus and connection across all areas of the school. By taking the most relevant leaves, the literacy team considered what these meant through the lens of literacy and built a network tree from the foundational elements of 'understanding'

and 'application' into the skills required at the word, sentence and text level. They framed these concepts with a continuum of skills from explicit teaching (foundational) through to the consideration of the skills being more than simply a way to achieve academic success, but the necessary life skills required as students left the college.

Figure 5.3: *WSLF* School Example #4 – The Literacy Link

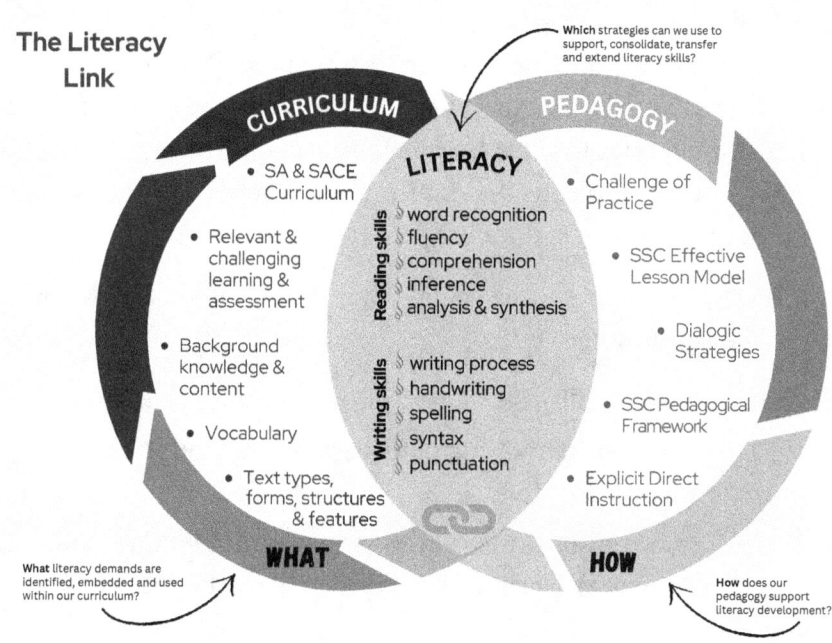

In this *Literacy Link* example, a co-educational government school had built a comprehensive pedagogical model and wanted to embed the literacy elements students were struggling with, without adding unnecessarily to the already extensive list of strategies and approaches teachers were grappling with. The 'Link' allowed the school to recognise how literacy was already embedded in everything they were doing, rather than a separate layer of skills and teaching required.

By continuing to focus on the curriculum and pedagogy areas the school was already working with, they were simply able to acknowledge and focus on understanding how literacy impacted the teaching and learning occurring within that curriculum or pedagogical area. Initially, the 'Link' was introduced to staff during a Curriculum Day, but follow-up was then focused on embedding a 'Link to Literacy' in every professional development session after this.

Drafting your Framework

Simply designing a pretty visual is obviously not enough. The importance of the *WSLF* design is in the semantics. You need to hold on to as much of the language your teachers are already using and capitalise upon ways to show how all the 'pieces' within the school fit together. You need to consider not simply the words you choose, but the relationship between different concepts being presented.

In this way, the focus for the initial development of your *WSLF* will involve brainstorming:

- the key literacy skills you want to prioritise across your school
- the language your school currently uses around literacy, curriculum and pedagogy
- the sequencing or priorities of the literacy skills identified and any supplementary learning skills that are priorities of focus to include
- where and how literacy 'sits' (or should sit) within the school in relation to other competing priorities.

There is no 'right' way to go about creating the Framework, but in general, the process is likely to involve the following steps:

1. **An initial discussion** about why the Framework would be beneficial for the school and who might be involved (see *Determining your literacy team* opposite)
2. **An audit** of the school's current practices, priorities, staff and student skills and knowledge, resources, time allocation,

available supports and potential budget (see *Key audit foci* on page 157)
3. **An initial brainstorm** sketching and drafting different elements, sequencing and synthesising concepts and overall vision
4. **An initial mock-up of the design** (or a couple of options) to take to the leadership team (or relevant staff) for feedback
5. **A redraft of the design** taking the feedback and practicalities into consideration
6. **A published introduction** to the staff more widely.

Determining your literacy team

Deciding on who will lead, support and be involved in the discussions around literacy will depend on the size of your school, the needs of the staff and students, the availability and willingness of staff, and the cost (of time and staffing). Often, a smaller group can be more efficient than a larger group, so you might consider the 'leading' team for literacy and then 'supporting' team members that assist in rolling it out across the school more broadly.

Leading team members might include:

- Literacy Leader
- Assistant/Deputy Principal or Director of Learning with a literacy portfolio
- English Head of Faculty/Department
- Literacy coaches/specialists.

I recommend, where possible, the Literacy Leader should *not* also be the Head of English. While they are often the most logical and experienced staff members to drive literacy development in a school, it is important that literacy is seen as *every* subject, not just something the English team is driving. The roots (or foundation) of literacy are found in English, so the English leader needs to be able to focus on the very large task of upskilling the English teachers at a much deeper level than the remaining staff members (see *Establishing the foundations* on page 175).

I would argue that there simply isn't enough time in the year for one person to support the work that needs to happen in the English Learning Area, as well as literacy more holistically across the school. Ideally, the Literacy Leader and the English HOD will work collaboratively, where the English HOD is setting up and ensuring literacy skills are being explicitly taught in English classes, and the Literacy Leader is setting up and ensuring the skills are being transferred, supported and extended in all the other classes across the school.

Supplementary team members might include:

- Curriculum or Teaching and Learning Leader
- Faculty or Department Leaders
- EAL/D Leader
- Librarian Leader
- Learning/Diversity/Educational Support Leader
- Critical friend/consultant/mentor/advisor
- Principal and any local or regional supervisors.

Any of these supplementary team members might be more relevant to include in the leading team, although these are the types of middle leadership roles that are most likely going to be used to support the implementation rather than plan and lead the initiative.

QUESTIONS TO CONNECT

- Who would be most relevant to include in the literacy team, and who would be supplementary members to support the decisions and work occurring?
- Of the members, who has the experience and position to make decisions, and what other external support may be required?
- When, and how often, would this team meet, and what would be their individual roles within the team?

Key audit foci

It is better to collect more (than less) information about the current (and historical) practices your school has around literacy and elements that impact literacy and learning. It is important to engage with a variety of staff while completing your audit, seeking different perspectives, recollections and opinions about what is currently happening, or has happened previously, across your school.

The following are some of the critical areas to explore:

- The school's professional development and meeting model, including staff groupings and time allocation. This will impact where literacy professional development might occur, how long the introduction and consolidation of information might take and where staff will have the opportunity to discuss, question and process information. This also allows you to consider the time available for staff to experiment in the classroom, build resources and revisions into the curriculum and engage with the information provided during professional development sessions.

- Other competing professional development and school-wide priorities that will either draw time away from literacy or can be connected with and supported through literacy.
- Opportunities for literacy connection, transference and consolidation across faculties and the community. What reading and writing demands are consistent or similar across faculties, and where are things read or written beyond the classroom?
- Where literacy sits in the school curriculum, staff online resources/shared folders and across the school more broadly. How do staff currently access literacy resources and information, and is it working?
- Previous and potential budget, considering things such as workshop presenters, resources, time allocation, etc.
- Current staff experience, confidence, motivations and understanding.
- Current student skills and behaviours as well as access to and engagement with literacy resources.
- Current language and approaches around literacy to hold on to, make consistent or consciously drop.
- Current intervention or support programs, their effectiveness and opportunities for extension or revision.

You can download a copy of a *Literacy Audit Questionnaire* in the appendices on page 195.

It is vital your school doesn't feel like it has to start from scratch when building its *WSLF*. Literacy has been taught across the school since the very beginning, and you need to acknowledge and build from this understanding, rather than reinventing the wheel, throwing the baby out with the bathwater or any other cliché that simply wastes teachers' time and energy.

Remember, we are not 'adding' literacy into classrooms, we are building staff and student capacity to continue to teach and learn *through* literacy.

As such, collating current language and approaches (even if they are currently either inconsistent or not embedded across the school) and considering ways to use this language in your Framework (and subsequent professional development) acknowledges to staff what they are already doing well. It means staff can see the *development* of literacy rather than adding to or 'starting again', and allows purposeful activation of professional prior knowledge rather than explicit teaching of new information to take place.

Just keep in mind that sometimes semantics are important. If one teacher introduces a case study expecting a formal extended essay and another expects a simple short answer response, students begin struggling to transfer their skills and knowledge, thinking what they are being asked to do is somehow completely different. Yet, sometimes, semantics don't matter. If the English department has been calling 'parts of speech' 'word classes', then as long as the language is consistent across the school, it doesn't matter what they are called. Go with what is currently being used. There is nothing worse than when teachers say, "So it's like such-and-such but just called something different…" This just wastes time and unnecessarily confuses everyone.

Once a draft of the Framework has been created, it is important to get feedback from key perspectives within your school. This doesn't necessarily mean taking it to the whole staff for consultation (although it can!), but the leadership team – and the faculty leaders if they aren't directly a part of the team – need to provide alternative perspectives around the language and approach being proposed. These will be the people who will ultimately action this Framework and see it play out, so ensuring they understand and approve the draft will be vital to its success.

QUESTIONS TO CONNECT

- How will an audit of your school take place, and who will be involved in collating and interpreting the results?
- Who will be involved in the initial brainstorming and drafting of the Framework?
- Who will mock up the initial design for the Framework?
- Who will provide feedback on the Framework draft, and who will decide on the final product?
- Is there a time frame for this process? *(Don't rush it: getting it right is more important than getting it done and then realising later that it doesn't work or needs revising.)*

Writing your Action Plan

Once the *WSLF* has been finalised, your school's literacy team must then, realistically, build a *Literacy Action Plan (LAP)* to strategically determine how the *WSLF* is going to be implemented. The *LAP* should take at least three years' foci into consideration and needs to identify the following elements:

- Clear literacy <u>objectives</u> (measurable vision statements) that broadly encapsulate the key focus areas for literacy improvement across the school
- Explicit <u>actions</u>, broken down into specific tasks for individuals to complete
- Identified <u>staff</u> to action each task, as well as those who will be involved
- The expected <u>timeline</u> for each event to either be completed or occur.

The analogy that creating change is a marathon, not a sprint, is never truer than in the context of a school that is working on embedding literacy. My argument is that if your school doesn't have an effective and workable curriculum to embed literacy into, then it is likely to be spinning in circles until it does (see *Literacy in the curriculum* on page 171). So, potentially, the first objective on your *LAP* might not involve any literacy-specific professional development for staff at all, but rather a considered focus on revising the curriculum and developing an approach that will then support the natural embedding of literacy as it is introduced.

Alternatively, your initial objective might be in the English faculty, ensuring that staff have the experience and skills, and are explicitly teaching the foundational elements required before you consider transferring and connecting the concepts and strategies across the school more holistically (see *Establishing the foundations* on page 175).

Generally, most *LAPs* will include objectives around:

- Staff professional development and induction processes
- Revising and embedding literacy into the curriculum
- The development, storage and use of literacy information and resources
- Collecting, interpreting and actioning student data
- English-specific auditing, curriculum revisions, scope and sequencing and English-specific professional development opportunities
- Literacy intervention and extension-specific programs and initiatives, including EAL/D programs
- Accountability, coaching and reflection points for processes enacted.

The important thing to remember when breaking down your objectives into <u>actions</u> is to be detailed and realistic. Just documenting that you will be running a workshop in Term 2, or want to set up a literacy folder in each faculty drive, doesn't help acknowledge the numerous individual steps required to action such tasks. The key here is to be highly *realistic* about how long things take to make, change or organise. Your *LAP* needs to balance everything you want to achieve within the confines of your role, time allocation and competing priorities.

An *Action Plan* should be built in a way to minimise overwhelm and maximise every opportunity for success.

If it is going to take two to three years before everything is properly set up and the foundations are ready before your school can even 'start' focusing on literacy, then that is always going to be the best (albeit frustrating!) process to begin.

Give yourself time to unpack and respond to the following critical questions to help determine your roll-out and sequencing of actions:

- What do your staff already know and what will they need to explicitly be taught?
- What sequence of learning will make the most logical sense for staff to engage with, and how long will that take?
- How will you *Check for Understanding* for each individual faculty and teacher, and how will you differentiate the learning to ensure maximum engagement and skill development?
- What time will you be able to provide, and how will you scaffold the revision of curriculum and resources to embed literacy purposefully and meaningfully?
- How quickly will you expect to 'see' literacy in the classroom, and what feedback and support will you offer teachers as they experiment with new strategies, approaches and language?
- What levels of accountability, flexibility and mentorship will you be able, or need, to apply?
- How will you induct new staff to 'catch up' and activate prior knowledge for returning staff each year on the learning that has occurred earlier?

Table 5.0 (overleaf) is a section from a school's initial *LAP*. It isn't wildly complex (nor should it be – it needs to be readable, actionable and useful), but it clearly highlights key objectives and actionable strategies the school is going to implement to achieve its objectives. The timelines inevitably changed along the way with the realities of a school, but the balancing of the different areas of focus can be seen and the clear actions helped build accountability by turning concepts into concrete, observable elements that could be reflected and built upon.

Establishing a *WSLF* and *LAP* is about being realistic and flexible. You know enough about the way schools function to acknowledge that best intentions don't necessarily mean things happen smoothly. You will have a far greater chance of success in improving literacy if you are realistic about how long it takes to be granted approval, collect feedback, upskill staff and build collective efficacy. Set yourself high and ambitious goals, but be honest about what it might take to achieve them.

QUESTIONS TO CONNECT

- What would be the key literacy objectives in your *LAP*?
- What would be the initial (and then subsequent) priority/ies within the plan?
- Realistically, how long will the initial stages of your plan take to enact?
- How will you engage with and revise your *LAP* along the way?

Table 5.0: Sample excerpt from school's *Literacy Action Plan*

Objective	Actions	People	Timeline
Provide explicit, purposeful and transferrable professional development across the college	Confirm, prepare and coordinate a WS PD *introducing the Framework* and the involvement of the staff moving forward. *Actions:* - Confirm schedule for the day - Book and confirm keynote presenter - Run faculty meeting to prep leaders for the day - Book hall and coordinate table set-up - Organise and publish table allocations - Email staff regarding expectations - Arrange printing resources Focus will be identifying the *literacy demands* of a subject-specific assessment task and considering ways to support these demands. *Following action:* Faculties to audit one assessment task per year level and revise to reflect literacy demands and strategies discussed	*Lead:* Lit. Leader *Facilitate:* Fac. Leaders *Present:* All staff	Curr Day Term 1
	Establish expectations and professional development specific to *English faculty* in relation to the *WSLF*. *Actions:* complete English *LAP* including: - Professional development opportunities - Resourcing and budget allocations - Curriculum auditing, development and sequencing of skills 7–12 - Correlation against the school *LAP* roll-out *Following action:* Confirm *LAP* with Literacy Team and begin actioning initial steps.	*HOD:* English Lit. Leader *Supported by:* Lit. Leader Eng. Faculty Lit. Consult	Term 1

Objective	Actions	People	Timeline
	Confirm and plan a Faculty Leaders' PD to model how to connect *writing process* into their faculty work and meetings in preparation for the Semester 2 WS PD. *Actions:* • Confer with Lit. Consult regarding key learning for WS PD and responsibilities for Fac. Leaders on the day • Prepare slide deck, handout and resources • Book meeting room • Email regarding expectations and link to shared folder *Following action:* Faculty leaders to decide what samples to look at (year-level subject – assessment and unit) at the WS PD and copy into Shared Folder.	*Lead:* Lit. Leader *Present:* Fac. Leaders *Supported by:* Lit. Consult	Fac. meet W2 T2
Embed teaching and learning practices into the curriculum	During Faculty Leader meetings: Reflective discussions about what content and details of the WS PD should translate into the subject-specific curriculum. *Actions:* • Lit. Leader to schedule and sequence literacy focus for faculties in correlation with WS Lit PD • Lit. Leader to confirm key questions, actions and discussions for faculties, at least one week prior to each faculty meeting. These should be able to be completed in no more than 20 minutes • Faculty Leaders to coordinate team and balance meeting agenda to include literacy content • Feedback and support to be presented through Faculty Leader meetings	Fac. Leaders *Supported by:* Lit. Leader	Throughout

Leading whole-school literacy 165

Objective	Actions	People	Timeline
	During PLC meetings: Specific literacy-focused Inquiry Cycle working in faculty and subject teams. *Actions:* • Key resources, templates, questions and support to be finalised by the end of Term 1 • PLC leaders to participate in literacy workshop (T1) in preparation for facilitating groups (T2) • Focus of PLC groups should align with faculty-specific literacy focus *Following action:* Presentation of PLC reflections to coincide with curriculum audit feedback and success sharing.	PLC Leaders All staff *Supported by:* Lit. Leader	Term 2
	Audit for appropriate and embedded literacy elements within curriculum documentation and classroom practice across the college. *Actions:* • Protocols and templates drafted and feedback provided through literacy and leadership team • Specific focus for learning walks determined three weeks prior and emailed to staff in advance • Curriculum audit focus and units of work determined at the start of each term and communicated with staff • Audit to occur in second-last week of term and feedback sent to faculty heads by end of term	Lit. Leader AP: Curric	LW = W5-6 Audit = end of terms
Establish protocols for the collection, interpretation and application of literacy data	Research, brainstorm and draft a proposal including: • What type of literacy data will be collected • Who will collect it and how • Who will interpret it • How the data will be shared • How the data will be expected to inform curriculum and teaching across the college	Lit. Leader AP: Curric AP: T&L HOD: English HOD: Learning Diversity	By the end of Term 4

Some leaders might prefer to translate this into a GAANT chart or other visual graphic to help see how timelines are realistic (or not) and how the different areas of focus are balanced across a term/year. A blank and editable *Action Plan* template can be downloaded from the appendices as well as a link to a GAANT chart template on page 195.

Beyond the curriculum day workshop

While a meaningful workshop, with time to discuss, explore and build resources on a staff curriculum day, can be highly effective and worthwhile, a full day often contains too much information for staff to process anyway. While you are planning when and how your professional development sessions are going to run, keep in mind how busy a teacher's life truly is and the ways you can make the learning as authentic, efficient and practical as possible.

Consider ways to build a culture of literacy within your school and how you can 'sprinkle' literacy through the year rather than focusing on it intensely for a year and then swapping to something else.

> "I will take a 10-minute spot every cycle in a staff meeting rather than a once-a-year full-day PD on literacy any day. Bite-sized consistency and purposeful retrieval practice will achieve significantly more than a prolonged but one-and-done approach every time" (Hayley Harrison*).

It is often the incidental discussions, explorations and resource-building activities throughout the year that are able to create the greatest consistency, build development and end up having significantly better impact upon a school than a full-day workshop – and they generally take less coordination, time and energy!

Be inspired by some of my favourite incidental ways to embed literacy across your school. Just keep in mind that your school will respond and connect with certain ideas differently than other contexts – so don't try to force an idea that is likely to fail… set yourself (and your staff) up for success.

---

* Speaking to every Literacy Leader she has ever worked with.

Incidental literacy activities

- **Connect non-literacy professional development back to the Literacy Framework purposefully.** If the Curriculum Leader can connect to where literacy fits, or the Teaching and Learning Leader can connect to how different pedagogical approaches can support reading and writing demands, or if the Principal can use some comprehension strategies when asking staff to read an article about positive school-wide behaviour, suddenly literacy becomes a part of the culture of the school.

- **Photocopier professional development** – display printed-out short activities, ideas or strategies in places where staff can read them incidentally; ideal places are near the photocopier, microwave, watercooler or any other spots that teachers find themselves waiting around looking for things to read! Change these reasonably regularly (once a week/cycle) and keep them super short and actionable.

- **One-page summaries** – share the professional reading, conferences and external workshops people have attended (in pigeonholes, on lunch tables, etc.).

- **Literacy bell-ringers or exit tickets 'gifts'** – these already-created subject-specific resources can be given directly to staff throughout the year. This is about acknowledging the time it can take to build resources, but popping a bow on an exit slip already printed and ready for a teacher to take into the classroom can be a more appreciated gift than chocolate for many teachers!

- **Word-of-the-day challenges** (for staff and students) – these can easily be added to a daily bulletin or school 'page', with online submissions to make it even easier to collate. The 'prizes' can be as simple as required, but a book, magazine or lovely pen are generally relevant 'literacy' prizes.

- **Literacy strategies posters** (comprehension and writing process, for example) – presenting the language of the school across the school reinforces the consistent language expectations and then PD can involve how to connect and use such resources in the classroom more purposefully.
- **Reading and writing goals** – these should be initially set in English but can then be documented in student diaries, and PD can involve how other teachers can refer to and connect these in their classes.
- **Teachers as writers** – teachers writing (creatively, persuasively, informatively, reflectively…) for the newsletter or staff anthology. This is particularly powerful when non-English teachers are published regularly.
- **Teacher book recommendations** (or 'what I am reading now') at the end of emails or displayed in the school – promotes lifelong literacy and opens conversations around reading and its impacts beyond the classroom.
- **Student-led newspaper/magazine** – less 'incidental' and certainly a significant amount of time and energy required, but this can be done on a smaller scale, published once a term and run by a different year level; or each class writes and publishes a page, etc.
- **Celebrating National Literacy/Book Week** – dates are set every year, but schools can select an appropriate time that suits them better if required. There are innumerable ways to develop literacy in engaging and powerful ways – which needn't involve getting dressed up as your favourite book character! (See options in the following box.)

NATIONAL LITERACY WEEK – ACTIVITIES

Literacy (or Book) Week can sometimes feel a little 'primary' if you let it, but these types of events can be amazing opportunities to celebrate and acknowledge literacy at a secondary level and the numerous ways literacy impacts our lives as adults.

Some ideas include:

- resume/application-writing workshops
- literacy 'did-you-know?' or challenges in daily bulletin
- What matters to me – rap/slam poetry/Ted Talk presentations
- Poetry on the Pavement (in chalk around school)
- author visits or writing workshops
- literacy quote badges (staff select their favourite to wear)
- staff versus student spelling competition
- community (or year level) book club
- comments added to Bookstagram, BookTube
- local library visit
- lunchtime read-aloud – with different 'guest' readers (Maths and PE teachers, for example)
- letter writing to a retirement village home
- primary school reading visit
- conversational English at a refugee centre
- book drive for remote communities
- literacy house competitions (poetry/micro fiction/spelling competitions)
- house or staff versus student debates
- AI writing competition.

You can download a copy of the *Literacy Quotes* (for Literacy Week badges) in the appendices on page 195.

Literacy in the curriculum

While the *WSLF* promotes longevity and development of staff capacity, the importance of embedding any literacy focus, understanding or strategy into a Guaranteed and Viable Curriculum cannot be ignored. While professional development can be given to new staff to come in line with literacy approaches (as part of a quality induction program), and retrieval practices can be used throughout the school calendar for staff more holistically, it is not until literacy is purposely embedded into an actionable curriculum that a school will be able to create lasting and increasing change.

Embedding literacy into the curriculum:

1. Reduces the cognitive load for teachers who are trying to balance competing factors in the classroom at any one time.
2. Supports the effectiveness of teaching, particularly for graduates, permission-to-teach, out-of-field and less experienced or confident teachers.
3. Allows schools to slowly introduce and experiment with unfamiliar skills and strategies without losing prior skills and strategies of focus.
4. Maximises the consistency across a school and evens the playing field of the 'teacher lottery' in which students can find themselves.
5. Provides the opportunity to evaluate if the curriculum is indeed overcrowded, lacking specificity or is unrealistic, and considers ways to prioritise and balance if required.
6. Holds teachers to some accountability to action the professional development and focus of the school into their classrooms. While this punitive approach is not its initial intention or priority, it is a way for a school to demonstrate what it wants to be seeing in classrooms and be well within its rights to then discuss if this is not occurring.

Each of these rationales is important enough in isolation, but it is the final cumulative approach to the building of teacher capacity that allows for the greatest impact to occur. By layering literacy skills into the curriculum as they are explicitly presented:

- teachers can see *how* the elements work together
- they are less overwhelmed or cognitively overloaded with how to organically draw the strategies into the classroom
- any new teachers to the school can see the processes and focus within the context of their subject's curriculum from the very beginning (with minimal training or support required).

But simply adding a list of vocabulary words, or a 'literacy column' to the edge of your unit plans, is not going to have the impacts highlighted above. It is important for Curriculum Leaders to recognise what is meant by 'embedding' literacy.

Table 5.1 highlights how *not* to include literacy in the curriculum and compares that against how it can be completed most effectively.

Table 5.1: Comparing effective and ineffective practices to embed literacy in the curriculum

Should NOT	Should
Be 'tacked onto' the start of the curriculum documentation or placed in a separate column alongside the lesson plan	Be purposefully embedded and connected with the reading or writing demands occurring in a lesson
Include a long list of vocabulary terms to teach within the lesson/week/unit that aren't connected to learning activities	Have key vocabulary embedded (and bolded) where it will be taught in the unit or lesson plan and appropriate strategies to support the vocabulary teaching and learning included throughout*
Add additional literacy-specific mini-lessons or literacy-specific activities to the lesson (outside of English, of course!)	Highlight where specific literacy approaches can best support the teaching of subject-specific content and skills (and mini-lessons embedded into English!)
Tokenistically flag activities as 'literacy' or 'literacy focus' in the curriculum without further support or specificity	Flag reading or writing demands with links to specific literacy strategies, approaches or relevant supports
Be a one-size-fits-all approach across every subject without the flexibility for subject-specific literacy demands to connect purposefully.	Be consistent with literacy metalanguage, expectations and approaches, but flexible with what this looks like depending on the subject.**

---

* Bolding words in curriculum documentation not only allows teachers to see where and how to consider new vocabulary but highlights when only technical (tier 3) words are being taught. A fascinating exercise can be to go through a unit of work and purposefully embed one academic (tier 2) word authentically into each lesson. It doesn't have to be explicitly taught, but it is an opportunity to consider when and how teachers can gift this language purposefully into their classes. These words can be simply identified using something like HSSW (see page 55), but if teachers aren't purposefully embedding this language into their lessons, when and how will it occur?

** English should approach literacy in the curriculum differently than Science; and Physical Education classes should approach literacy differently in its practical classes than it does in theory classes, for example.

Connect: from page to practice

Start actioning your learning! Determine the key team members who will be involved in developing and facilitating the literacy changes across your school and then:

1. Audit current practices, priorities and perspectives.
2. Draft a Whole-School Literacy Framework.
3. Establish the priorities.
4. Backwards map to develop a *Literacy Action Plan* (ensuring that you include *all* key areas of focus, not just the teacher-facing professional development opportunities).
5. Start actioning the *Literacy Action Plan* and see what is truly possible at your school.

Remember: I made this sound easy, but you just need to take one step at a time, knowing that if you plan properly, you have set yourself up for success. You will have to be painstakingly patient and consistent, but if you get the planning right and think about the long-term vision, then I promise it is not only possible, but more than achievable!

Establishing the foundations: English priorities

The importance of establishing Year 7 as a foundational year for consolidating a consistent understanding of literacy skills and language cannot be undervalued in a secondary context. While some schools do have students move from Year 6 into Year 7 within the make-up of their school, predominantly, Year 7 is a mix of new students coming from a wide variety of experiences. The scheduling of separate classes and teachers is also significantly different from the literacy blocks they often experienced in primary school.

Establishing the 'language' of your school, regarding reading, writing, speaking and listening to the English language, allows schools to maximise the opportunity to 'get everyone on the same page'. Once foundational language and skills have been explicitly taught (or prior knowledge has been activated and consolidated), then subject teachers can be confident to use the technical language around literacy in their classes and the feedback they provide.

While it is possible to categorise this language and subsequent skills into reading, writing, speaking or listening, so many elements cross between modes as the language we use to communicate, and as such I find it more useful to categorise them into foundational understanding and skills of *sentences, language, reading* and *writing*, as seen in Figure 5.4 overleaf.

Figure 5.4: Foundational skills and knowledge

Foundational skills and knowledge

Foundations of a sentence
- subject and predicate/verb
- clauses and phrases
- sentence barrier punctuation

Foundations of language
- parts of speech (*focus on function rather than labels*)
- speech versus written expression (*syntax / language features*)
- punctuation for purpose and effect
- spelling and vocabulary (*morphology, orthography, denotation, connotation*)

Foundations of reading
- comprehension strategies (*at word, sentence, text level*)
- decoding/fluency *(if required)*
- stamina and reading for purpose (*text types, forms / audience*)
- synthesising and analytical thinking (*using evidence to support*)

Foundations of writing
- the writing process (*strategies for pre, during and post*)
- writing for purpose and audience (*structures and features*)
- register and voice
- handwriting and typing (*if required*)

You can download a copy of a *Literacy Skills and Knowledge Checklist* in the appendices on page 195.

This explicit literacy teaching should be prioritised in either the English curriculum or a separate literacy-specific subject (that is consolidated in English). The way you will plan to teach these things, however, will look very different depending on whether you are using a literacy block or solely the English classes to teach these skills.

Table 5.2 highlights the flexibility that a literacy block can offer to sequence, explicitly teach and experiment with language foundations, without the confines of competing with an assessable curriculum. Remember that students need to actively *transfer* these skills and see the benefit of this class, though. A once-a-week, unassessed class is often less effective than putting the expectations more purposefully into the English curriculum, but it can also ensure teachers don't deprioritise literacy in the often-overcrowded English curriculum they must navigate.

Table 5.2: Example plan of sequenced skills for a Year 7 literacy-specific block

Term One	Term Two	Term Three	Term Four
Foundations of our language	Reading and writing for purpose	Language over time	Strategies to support myself
• subject and predicate • end marks and capital letters • modifiers • 4 components of spelling • handwriting	• clauses and phrases • punctuating quotes • punctuating dialogue • commas • conjunctions • creative spelling • academic v technical vocabulary	• denotation v connotation • history of spelling (etymology) • spoken v written syntax • subject verb agreement • cohesive ties	• fixing fragment/run on sentences • apostrophes • subject verb agreement • morphology and the impact on vocabulary development

Leading whole-school literacy

While there are some benefits to streaming such literacy-specific classes, it is important to recognise how such approaches can widen the gap in skills and knowledge, rather than reduce it. Jiban (2025) argues that ability-levelled classes can become an equity issue if teachers "don't grant [students] access to grade level texts". This supports the perspective that every student deserves the opportunity to experience the same content and skills through school; they will simply require different scaffolds to either support or extend a text or task depending on the abilities of the student. When below-level students are only given access to below-level texts, they "miss the rich and varied vocabulary and syntax" they need to understand and build the sophistication and complexity increasingly required through school and beyond.

Whether foundational literacy is embedded within the English curriculum or a stand-alone literacy class, it must be a priority for English teachers to embed the language and skills into their curriculum and lead the way in supporting and extending students in their linguistic awareness and understanding.

Table 5.3 considers where the foundational skills could be embedded into different units across the curriculum in Year 7 English. Notice how many skills are given more than one opportunity for explicit teaching, but also how many elements need to be considered within any particular unit of work. Expecting teachers to subconsciously or organically remember to balance these many collaborative factors alongside an already full curriculum is unrealistic; it requires focused time to audit and embed such elements purposefully throughout.

Table 5.3: Example plan for embedding literacy skills in Year 7 English units

Term One	Term Two	Term Three	Term Four
Writing for purpose	Persuasive analysis	Text analysis	Poetry analysis
<ul><li>end marks and capital letters</li><li>punctuating dialogue</li><li>subject and predicate</li><li>noun and verb phrases</li><li>history of spelling</li><li>handwriting?</li></ul>	<ul><li>punctuating quotes</li><li>commas</li><li>clauses and phrases</li><li>subject verb agreement</li><li>academic v technical vocabulary</li><li>handwriting?</li></ul>	<ul><li>punctuating quotes</li><li>commas</li><li>fixing fragments</li><li>cohesive devices: conjunctions</li><li>denotation v connotation</li><li>spelling: adding suffixes</li><li>handwriting?</li></ul>	<ul><li>punctuating quotes</li><li>apostrophes</li><li>denotation v connotation</li><li>cohesive ties</li><li>etymology and morphology and the impact on spelling</li></ul>
	Persuasive writing		Poetry writing
	<ul><li>noun and verb phrases</li><li>cohesive devices: conjunctions</li><li>spoken v written language features</li><li>spelling 'silent e'</li><li>handwriting?</li></ul>		<ul><li>using clauses and phrases for creative effect</li><li>cohesive ties: for creative effect</li><li>affixes: prefixes and suffixes</li><li>handwriting?</li></ul>

Embedding, rather than dedicating a grammar or literacy-specific lesson, will have greater impact for students' transference of skills, but this requires staff to *prioritise* the literacy teaching and learning rather than see it as an optional extra or only if they have time. It also requires staff to have greater confidence in understanding and using the language around grammar more purposefully. For many English faculties and teachers, this will require significant professional development and support. Initially, schools may need to consider how they ensure grammar and foundational literacy are being taught consistently and slowly work towards integrating such elements more authentically as the skills of their teachers increase.

Just as you will need to embed literacy concepts and strategies into the curriculum across the school, you will need to embed the grammatical concepts and language into the English curriculum. The better you can show how to integrate the teaching, through mini-lessons, activation of prior knowledge, and the consolidation of skills through content learning and application within the curriculum, the more likely it is that teachers will be able to teach the skills purposefully and students will be able to understand and apply the skills.

As the Literacy Leader, you can't ask your Science teachers to experiment with appositive phrases in their classes if the English teacher hasn't explicitly taught what a pronoun or a phrase is in the first place. Therefore, ensuring the English teachers have the necessary skills to teach literacy and that these skills are embedded within the English curriculum explicitly must be a priority for any school trying to focus on and improve literacy for their students. As previously noted, it might mean that the initial time and energy of your *LAP* is actually limited to your English department before extending out to the rest of the school.

QUESTIONS TO CONNECT

- How confident are the English teachers at your school to diagnose, explicitly teach, scaffold and extend foundational literacy skills within the English curriculum?

- Where are the foundational language skills being taught, consolidated and extended at Year 7*, and how are these transferred into other subjects and contexts?

- What resources, supports and experience do you have (or need) within the English department?

- What literacy areas do students at your school generally struggle with the most, and how does the current curriculum design support the explicit teaching, consolidation and extension of these skills specifically?

---

* If your school does not begin at Year 7, but your first student intake is at Year 9 (or above), the concept of establishing a consistent language for students to transfer into all subjects still applies. However, this might prioritise *Activating Prior Knowledge* and setting up the language of the school more broadly during Term 1, rather than a clear scope and sequence of explicit teaching. Instead of assuming student knowledge, acknowledge that different schools and teachers might have slightly different language to discuss the same concepts, and be prepared to explicitly teach what a sentence is at Year 11 – I'm yet to find a class that didn't need a refresher (or an introduction!) to help establish the language and be able to build from throughout the year.

Leading Whole-School Literacy... in summary

The problem with literacy PD
Any literacy professional development needs to consider not only the complexity and number of literacy skills that can be focused upon, but the diversity of both student and staff literacy knowledge and skills.

Embedding into the curriculum
One of the most important elements to build capacity, longevity, consistency and development is to purposefully and explicitly embed each literacy element into the school's actively used curriculum.

Incidental literacy
Beyond literacy-specific professional development, schools can consider a variety of ways to build literacy into the language and culture of their school including different activities, priorities and celebrations.

Developing the WSLF

While there is no 'right' way to build a *Whole-School Literacy Framework*, it is important to take the time to consider all elements before presenting it to staff.

Key processes should include:
1. An initial discussion to determine the literacy team, as well as the time and resources initially available
2. A comprehensive audit of the school's current practices, priorities, resources, budget as well as staff and student skills and knowledge
3. An initial brainstorm, sketching and drafting of the design to take for feedback
4. Redrafting, publication and Action Plan writing.

Developing the *LAP*

The *Literacy Action Plan* is a way to balance the number of focus points with the scope and sequencing of priorities.
The *LAP* should identify:
- Clear literacy objectives and the key focus areas across the school
- Explicit actions for each area
- Specific staff (or roles) to complete or be involved in identified actions
- An expected timeline or order of completion.

Foundational English

While literacy needs to be a whole-school focus, a literacy plan should always consider the importance of diagnosing, establishing and explicitly teaching literacy in English. Initially, this will be foundational and explicit in Year 7, and then sequenced across subsequent year levels to consolidate and extend towards senior years.

Connecting Whole-School Literacy in the Secondary Context

Conclusion

Literacy is complex. No one is ever going to deny that fact.

Working with teenagers is highly complex. No one could ever possibly deny that fact!

But teachers are pretty amazing creatures, who choose to work with these volatile humans, en masse, in close quarters every day and have to use literacy to communicate with them.

And *that* is either insanity or heroic (possibly a bit of both).

Reading this book hasn't made literacy or teenagers any less complex, but my intention was to highlight *why* literacy is complex (because knowledge always equals power), and to present a few key concepts and strategies that might lessen the challenge of dealing with the literacy demands of your students.

So, what am I hoping you are walking away with after investing your precious time and mental energy in consuming these words?

1. Every teacher needs to be the expert in the subject-specific literacy demands of whatever subject they are teaching. This not only involves the technical language or background content knowledge, but the specific structures and language features used to read, speak and write like a historian/scientist/musician/electrician/designer/mathematician/(insert your subject here).
2. When teaching vocabulary, teachers need to consider more than simply the technical words required in their subject, but the academic and descriptive language that is used around

the technical language. They also need to ensure students not only understand the <u>definition</u> and meaning of a word, but the potential <u>connotation</u> as well as be able to <u>pronounce, spell and change the function</u> of a word so they can use it correctly and effectively as part of their active vocabulary.

3. Reading (generally) occurs in a student's mind, so it is important for a teacher to have a variety of ways to <u>assess student understanding and comprehension</u> of a text. When misunderstanding occurs, teachers need to have strategies to support students at the <u>word, sentence or text level</u>, depending on where the student has become confused.

4. Writing requires <u>more cognitive load</u>, and therefore effort, than reading and requires students to draw from their long-term memory at the same time as holding numerous elements in their working memory. Writing is, however, one of the most common ways students' understanding of content is assessed, so teachers need to be able to differentiate between a student who has misunderstood the content and a student who doesn't have the writing skills to articulate their understanding. Having different strategies to build student writing skills, in conjunction with and <u>as a way to teach the content</u>, maximises students' ability not only to process new information and retain it, but also to transfer writing skills across units, subjects and years.

Finally, I couldn't write this text without speaking to and supporting the leaders who have been assigned the epic task of 'improving literacy' at their school. The array of competing priorities, the limited time, the extreme differences in experience, knowledge and skills doesn't balance well against the fact that a school can never 'achieve' literacy. Your school will not reach a point where it has completed its focus on literacy, but it is something that can always be improved, refined and extended. As such, leaders need to be prepared for an endless cycle and future that involves literacy.

Rather than feel even more overwhelmed by such a task, I am hoping that leaders have found a way into and through literacy professional development and potential literacy connections within the context of their school and that teachers have clarified their understanding of literacy and can see how to engage with it purposefully in the context of their specific classroom.

Literacy will, and should, look different in different schools, but ultimately, I am hoping that after reading Chapter 5, leaders with literacy in their portfolio will be excited to:

- engage in auditing the current practices and opportunities of their school
- explore different ways to establish a vision for literacy that can stand the test of time and any future changes in leadership and priorities
- be prepared to cover everything, but remain realistic in how to plan for a roll-out that supports rather than overwhelms
- work with the English department on ensuring the foundations of literacy and the language around literacy are established effectively, purposefully and sequenced in a way to consolidate and extend students throughout their journey at the school.

I recognise that not everyone will be quite so passionate about literacy as I am, and that is OK. You don't have to love literacy – but you do need to respect it.

Respect it for its complexity as well as its power to change a student's life.

Respect it for the impact it has in your classroom and your life more broadly.

Respect it for what it has offered you in life and how you can gift its power to every student who comes before you.

I genuinely can't wait to hear the success you uncover in unlocking student potential through a focus on literacy. Just know you are not alone. You don't have to have all the answers. We learn more from experimenting and getting things wrong, and literacy is the one thing you can always rely on. I promise.

Literacy and justice for all.

Hayley

References

Adoniou, M. (2022). *Spelling it Out: How Words Work & How to Teach Them* (Revised edition). Cambridge University Press.

Albright, J., Knezevic L., & Farrell, L. (2013). Everyday practices of teachers of English: A survey at the outset of national curriculum implementation. *The Australian Journal of Language and Literacy, 36*(2): 111–120.

Alexander, R. (2012). *Improving Oracy and Classroom Talk in English Schools: Achievements and Challenges*. Cambridge University Press.

Alexander, R. (2020). *A Dialogic Teaching Companion*. Routledge.

Art of Smart. (2025). The Complete HSC English Visual Techniques Cheat Sheet. https://artofsmart.com.au/english/visual-techniques/

Australian Curriculum, Assessment and Reporting Authority (ACARA). (n.d.). *The Australian Curriculum*. Version 9.0. https://v9.australiancurriculum.edu.au/

Beck, I. L., McKeown, M. G., & Kucan, L. (2013). *Bringing Words to Life: Robust Vocabulary Instruction*. Guilford Press.

Berninger, V. W., Vaughan, K., Abbott, R. D., Begay, K., Coleman, K. B., Curtin, G., Hawkins, J. M., & Graham, S. (2002). Teaching spelling and composition alone and together: Implications for the simple view of writing. *Journal of Educational Psychology, 94*(2), 291–304.

Berninger, V. W., & Winn, W. D. (2006). Implications of Advancements in Brain Research and Technology for Writing Development, Writing Instruction, and Educational Evolution. In C. A. MacArthur, S. Graham, & J. Fitzgerald (Eds.), *Handbook of Writing Research* (pp. 96–114). Guilford Press.

Bolton, L. (2020). Bridging the Word Gap at transition: The Oxford Language Report 2020. Oxford Education. Oxford University Press. https://educationblog.oup.com/secondary/english/the-oxford-language-report-2020-bridging-the-word-gap-at-transition

Bosse, M.-L., Tainturier, M.-J, & Valdois, S. (2007). Developmental dyslexia: The visual attention span hypothesis. *Cognition, 104*(2), 198–230.

Castro, N. (2023). How Does Your Brain Remember and Retrieve Words? *Scientific American*. https://www.scientificamerican.com/article/how-does-your-brain-remember-and-retrieve-words/

Dale, E. (1965). Vocabulary Measurement: Techniques and Major Findings. *Elementary English, 42*(8), 895–901, 948.

Dean, N. (2019). A Look at the Write Brain. *BrainWorld Magazine*.

Derewianka, B. (1994). *A Grammar Companion*. Primary English Teaching Association.

de Zubicaray, G. (2023). Is it normal to forget words while speaking? And when can it spell a problem? *The Conversation*, https://theconversation.com/is-it-normal-to-forget-words-while-speaking-and-when-can-it-spell-a-problem-212852

Didau, D. (2020). *The Secret of Literacy: Making the Implicit, Explicit*. Independent Thinking Press.

Doug, R. (2019). Handwriting: Developing Pupils' Identity and Cognitive Skills. *International Journal of Education & Literacy Studies*, 7(2), 177–188.

EAP Foundation. (n.d.). The Academic Vocabulary List (AVL). https://www.eapfoundation.com/vocab/academic/other/avl/

EAP Foundation. (n.d.). The Academic Word List (AWL). https://www.eapfoundation.com/vocab/academic/awllists/

Ehri, L.C. (2014). Orthographic Mapping in the Acquisition of Sight Word Reading, Spelling Memory, and Vocabulary Learning. *Scientific Studies of Reading*, 18(1), 5–21.

Eide, D. (2012). *Uncovering the Logic of English: A Common-Sense Approach to Reading, Spelling, and Literacy*. Logic of English.

Fiveable. (n.d.) Salience of Features. https://library.fiveable.me/key-terms/cognitive-psychology/salience-of-features

Gentry, J. R., & Graham, S. (2010). *Creating Better Readers and Writers: The Importance of Direct, Systematic Spelling and Handwriting Instruction in Improving Academic Performance*. Saperstein Associates.

Goss, P., & Sonnemann, J. (2016). Widening gaps: What NAPLAN tells us about student progress. https://grattan.edu.au/report/widening-gaps/

Gough, P. B., & Tunmer, W. E. (1986). Decoding, Reading, and Reading Disability. *Remedial and Special Education*, 7(1), 6–10.

Graves, M. F. (2006). *The Vocabulary Book: Learning & Instruction*. Teachers College Press.

Harrison, H. (2022). *Connecting Literacy Teacher Book 1*. Matilda Education.

Harrison, H. (2022). *Connecting Literacy Teacher Book 2*. Matilda Education.

Harrison, H. (2022). *Connecting Literacy Teacher Book 3*. Matilda Education.

Hochman, J. C., & Wexler, N. (2017). *The Writing Revolution*. Jossey-Bass.

Jerrim, J., & Moss, G. (2019). The link between fiction and teenagers' reading skills: International evidence from the OECD PISA study. *British Educational Research Journal*, 45(1), 181–200.

Jiban, C. (2025). Let's talk equity: Reading levels, scaffolds, and grade-level text. NWEA. https://www.nwea.org/blog/2025/equity-in-reading-levels-scaffolds-and-grade-level-text/#

Kiliç, M. (2019). Vocabulary Knowledge as a Predictor of Performance in Writing and Speaking. *PASSA*, 57, 1–32.

Knoph, R. E., Lawrence, J. F., & Francis, D. J. (2024). The Dimensionality of Lexical Features in General, Academic, and Disciplinary Vocabulary. *Scientific Studies in Reading*, 28(2), 142–166.

Lawrence, J. (2021). What can the simple view of reading teach us about disciplinary literacy? Reading Ways. https://tinyurl.com/2knjcf8u

Lehr, F., Osborn, J., & Hiebert, E. H. (2005). *A Focus on Comprehension* (Research-Based Practices in Early Reading Series). Regional Educational Laboratory: Pacific Resources for Education and Learning.

Lynch, A. (2009). Changing Schools: How Policy Implementation Can Impact on the Literacy Learning of Mobile Students. *Australasian Journal of Early Childhood, 34*(2), 47–53.

Marzano, J. (2005). *Building Academic Background Knowledge*. Association for Supervision and Curriculum Development, Alexandria.

McCallum, A. (2025). Bringing the Fiction Effect into Schools. English & Media Centre. https://www.englishandmedia.co.uk/blog/bringing-the-fiction-effect-into-schools/

McLean, E., & Griffiths, K. (2024). Writing and writing instruction. Australian Education Research Organisation. https://www.edresearch.edu.au/research/research-reports/writing-and-writing-instruction

Merga, M. K. (2023). *Creating an Australian School Literacy Policy: A Research-Informed Guide to Designing a Policy That Fits Your School*. Hawker Brownlow Education.

Miller, G. A., & Gildea, P. M. (1987). How children learn words. *Scientific American, 257*(3), 94–9.

Moats, L. C. (2005). How Spelling Supports Reading: And why it is more regular and predictable than you may think. *American Educator*: Winter 2005/06.

Montgomery, P., Ilk, M., & Moats, L. C. (2012). *A Principal's Primer for Raising Reading Achievement*. Sopris Learning.

Murphy, J., & Murphy, D. (2019). *Thinking Reading*. John Catt Educational Ltd.

Organisation for Economic Co-operation and Development (OECD). (2019). *Skills Matter: Additional Results from the Survey of Adult Skills*. OECD Skills Studies, OECD Publishing.

Oxford English Dictionary. (n.d.). Literacy. https://www.oxfordlearnersdictionaries.com/definition/english/literacy?q=literacy

Oxford Learners Dictionaries. (n.d.). Oxford 3000 and 5000. https://www.oxfordlearnersdictionaries.com/wordlists/oxford3000-5000

Quigley, A. (2018). *Closing the Vocabulary Gap*. Routledge.

Quigley, A. (2020). *Closing the Reading Gap*. Routledge.

Quigley, A. (2022). *Closing the Writing Gap*. Routledge.

Reed, D. K. (2012). Why Teach Spelling? Portsmouth, NH: RMC Research Corporation, Center on Instruction.

Resnick, L. B., Asterhan, C. S. C., & Clarke, S. N. (2018). Accountable talk: Instructional dialogue that builds the mind. UNESCO. *Educational Practices Series, 29*(61). https://unesdoc.unesco.org/ark:/48223/pf0000262675

Rutherford, L., Singleton, A., Reddan, B., Johanson, K., & Dezuanni, M. (2024). *Discovering a Good Read: Exploring Book Discovery and Reading for Pleasure Among Australian Teens*. Deakin University.

Salmerón, L., Vargas, C., Delgado, P., & Baron, N. (2023). Relation between digital tool practices in the language arts classroom and reading comprehension scores. *Reading and Writing, 36*(1):175–194.

Scali, J. (2023). High Impact Reading Instruction and Intervention in the Primary Years. Amba Press.

Sedita, J. (2023). *The Writing Rope: A Framework for Explicit Writing Instruction in All Subjects.* Paul H. Brookes Publishing Co.

Shanahan, T. (2018). Comprehension Skills or Strategies: Is there a difference and does it matter? Shanahan on Literacy [blog]. https://tinyurl.com/3u9876ez

Share, D. L. (2008). Orthographic Learning, Phonological Recoding, and Self-Teaching. *Advances in Child Development and Behavior, 36,* 31–82.

Spichtig, A. N., Pascoe, J. P., Gehsmann, K. M., Gu, F., & Ferrara, J. D. (2022). The Interaction of Silent Reading Rate, Academic Vocabulary, and Comprehension Among Students in Grades 2–12. *Reading Research Quarterly, 57*(1).

Swanborn, M. S. L., & de Glopper, K. (1999). Incidental word learning while reading: A meta-analysis. *Review of Educational Research, 69*(3), 261–285.

Tam, K. (2017). The Impact of Poor Literacy in School Students. Lynn's Learning. https://www.lynnslearning.com.au/impact-poor-literacy-school-students/

The Reading and Writing Hotline. (2020). Helping Clients Fill in Forms Report. Social Equity Works.

Walker, L. & Bayetto, A. (2021). The language gap in Australian students' writing. Oxford Children's Language. https://www.oup.com.au/__data/assets/pdf_file/0026/174851/PRIM_LanguageGapReport_2021_LOWRES-002.pdf

Welsh, J., Bishop, K., Booth, H., Butler, D., Gourley, M., Law, H. D., Banks, E., Canudas-Romo, V., & Korda, R. J. (2021). Inequalities in life expectancy in Australia according to education level: A whole-of-population record linkage study. *International Journal for Equity in Health, 20*(1):178.

Wharton, T. (2023). Visual Language Features in the English Curriculum. Twinkl. https://www.twinkl.com.au/blog/visual-language-features-in-the-english-curriculum

Wiley, R. W., & Rapp, B. (2021). The effects of handwriting experience on literacy learning. *Psychological Science, 32*(7), 1086–1103.

Willis, J. (2011). The Brain-Based Benefits of Writing for Math and Science Learning. Edutopia. https://www.edutopia.org/blog/writing-executive-function-brain-research-judy-willis

Wolf, M. (2008). *Proust and the Squid: The Story and Science of the Reading Brain.* Icon Books.

List of figures and tables

Figures

Figure 1.0: Literacy as a competence and knowledge of a specific area	14
Figure 1.1: Elements impacting text complexity	21
Figure 1.2: Example layout of the classroom set-up for a *Socratic Circle* discussion	28
Figure 2.0: Brain areas related to the skill of comprehension and reading	40
Figure 2.1: The similar skills required to decode and encode unfamiliar words	41
Figure 2.2: Active and passive vocabulary	45
Figure 2.3: The Three Tiers of Vocabulary	48
Figure 2.4: The *HSSW* model	55
Figure 2.5: Example *SEA It* Ticket	59
Figure 2.6: Example *10 Most Important Words* table	63
Figure 2.7: Example *Word Matrix*	66
Figure 2.8: Example *Word Builder*	67
Figure 2.9: Example *Frayer Model*	68
Figure 2.10: Example *Word Investigation*	69
Figure 2.11: Example *Word Clarifying* worksheet	70

Figure 3.0: *The Simple View of Reading* formula — 74

Figure 3.1: *The Simple View of Writing* formula — 74

Figure 3.2: *The Reading Rope* graphic — 75

Figure 4.0: *The Writing Rope* — 108

Figure 4.1: The Simple View of Writing and its transition into The Not-So-Simple View of Writing model — 109

Figure 4.2: The essential elements of the writing process — 127

Figure 5.0: *WSLF* School Example #1 – The Layers of Literacy — 150

Figure 5.1: *WSLF* School Example #2 – The Literacy Arc — 151

Figure 5.2: *WSLF* School Example #3 – The Literacy Branch — 152

Figure 5.3: *WSLF* School Example #4 – The Literacy Link — 153

Figure 5.4: Foundational skills and knowledge — 176

Tables

Table 1.0: Comparing the subskills of reading and writing — 15

Table 1.1: Potential vocabulary, reading and writing demands in subjects across secondary school — 22

Table 1.2: Comparing the processes involved in speaking and listening, and in reading and writing — 25

Table 1.3: *Accountable Talk* example sentence starters — 27

Table 1.4: Alternative *Third Move* responses for varying effect — 30

Table 2.0: Common command terms used in secondary settings — 49

Table 3.0: Subject-specific reading skills, categorised into *Reading Rope* subskills — 78

Table 3.1: Potential reading forms in a secondary context — 80

Table 3.2: Example Question Creation Table — 104

Table 4.0: Potential writing forms — 124

Table 4.1: Comparing the expectations of the writing process for different text forms	128
Table 4.2: Potential strategies for each stage of the writing process	129
Table 5.0: Sample excerpt from a school's *Literacy Action Plan*	164
Table 5.1: Comparing effective and ineffective practices to embed literacy in the curriculum	173
Table 5.2: Example plan of sequenced skills for a Year 7 literacy-specific block	177
Table 5.3: Example plan for embedding literacy skills in Year 7 English units	179

Appendices

Downloadable resources

- '...in summary' graphics from each chapter
- *Activating Prior Knowledge* activities
- *Common Academic Words* list
- *Common Command Terms* list
- *Common Prefixes* (and their meanings) list
- *Common Suffixes* (and their meanings) list
- *Comprehension Strategies Handout*
- *HSSW* graphic
- *Literacy Quotes* (for Literacy Week badges)
- *Literacy Skills and Knowledge* checklist
- *Reading* and *Writing Ropes* graphics
- *Sea It* Ticket graphic
- *Spelling Strategies* graphic
- *Strategies Across the Writing Process* table
- *Text Complexity Variables* graphic

Downloadable resources: editable blank copies

- *10 Most Important Words* table
- *Action Plan* template
- *All the Words Around* worksheet
- English Curriculum Overview table
- *LAP GAANT* Chart template
- *Gallery Walk* handout
- *Literacy Audit Questionnaire*
- Literacy Demands table
- *Question Creation Table*
- *Selection of Writing Organisers*
- *Selection of Reading Organisers*
- *Word Builder* worksheet
- *Word Clarifying* worksheet
- *Word Investigation* worksheet
- *Writing Process Expectations* table

Recommended further reading and resources

- *Spelling it Out* by Misty Adoniou
- *Bringing Words to Life* by Isabel Beck, Margaret McKeown and Linda Kucan
- *A Grammar Companion* by Beverley Derewianka
- *The Secret of Literacy* by David Didau
- *Connecting Literacy [1, 2 and 3]* by Hayley Harrison
- *The Writing Revolution* by Judith Hochman and Natalie Wexler
- *Thinking Reading* by James and Dianne Murphy
- *Closing the Reading Gap* by Alex Quigley
- *Closing the Vocabulary Gap* by Alex Quigley
- *Closing the Writing Gap* by Alex Quigley

Index

Accountable Talk 26, 27, 32, 138
Active Listening 31, 32, 151
active vocabulary 37, 44, 45, 46, 48, 50, 54, 58, 64, 72, 111, 117, 184
annotations 90, 98, 119
appositive 97, 132, 133, 135, 180

bell-ringer activities 58, 65, 112, 168

Check for Understanding 83, 84, 118, 162
clause 87, 131, 134, 176, 177, 179
cognitive load 21, 43, 107, 147, 171, 184
cohesive device 96, 119, 150, 152, 179
cohesive tie 135, 142, 177, 179
command (or instructional) words 49, 50, 51, 72, 150
comprehension 24, 37, 40, 43, 45, 73, 81, 83, 96, 98, 123, 176, 184

conjunctions 87, 96, 119, 134, 137, 177, 179
connectives 87, 96, 97, 101, 106, 119, 120, 137

decode 40, 41, 42, 44, 46, 72, 75, 92, 93
denotation 64, 176, 177, 179
dependent sentences 134
derivations 57, 64

encode 40, 41, 43, 44, 72
etymology/etymological 117, 177, 179
exit slip 58, 65, 103, 112, 168

foundational literacy skills 6, 178, 179, 181
fronted adverbial 131

grammar 6, 15, 25, 108, 130, 152, 179

handwriting 6, 15, 68, 108, 115, 121, 122, 125, 130, 142, 153, 176, 177, 179

independent sentences 119

language processing 74, 107, 108, 109
literacy demand 7, 13, 17, 20, 21, 23, 33, 145, 153, 164, 173, 183

mental lexicon 42, 43, 46
morphology/morphological/morphological awareness 41, 56, 65, 108, 117, 150, 176, 177, 179

Note Making 90, 91, 98, 101, 106

objectives 160, 161, 163, 164, 165, 166, 182
oral literacy 7, 24, 25, 151
orthography/orthographical/orthographic mapping 15, 43, 45, 46, 48, 50, 56, 60, 72, 75, 106, 115, 117, 176

partial mapping 45
passive vocabulary 44, 45, 47, 72, 111, 112
phonemic awareness 41, 92
phonology/phonological awareness 56, 75, 106, 108

phrase 87, 93, 131, 132, 135, 176, 177, 179, 180
pronouns 96, 97, 106, 119, 132, 135, 137, 180
punctuation 6, 15, 19, 42, 68, 75, 93, 99, 108, 113, 114, 120, 125, 128, 130, 142, 153, 176

retrieval practice 19, 46, 58, 103, 111, 167, 171

Socratic Circles 28, 151
spelling 15, 41, 43, 56, 64, 108, 115, 125, 176
subject (grammatical reference) 42, 87, 97, 119, 135, 176
Subject-Specific Literacy 13, 20, 21, 33, 173, 183
subordinate conjunction 134
syntactic system/awareness 19, 42

Three Tiers of Vocabulary 47, 48, 72
transcription 74, 107, 108, 109

writing complexity 125